JOTUNHEIM

VANAHEIM

SVARTALFHEIM

NIFLHEIM

THE OFFICIAL COOKBOOK
OF THE NINE REALMS

GOD OF WAR™

THE OFFICIAL COOKBOOK
OF THE NINE REALMS

BY VICTORIA ROSENTHAL
AND RICK BARBA

ILLUSTRATIONS BY IRIS COMPIET

TITAN
BOOKS
LONDON

CONTENTS

FOREWORD

> "Týr believed the mind, not might, was key to preventing war and chaos. And he also knew visiting other cultures would give him perspective staying in one place could not. While Odin always hoarded knowledge, guarding it jealously, Týr was open and sharing with his learning and his wisdom."

—Mimir, *God of War* (2018)

Visiting cultures.
Broad perspectives.
Sharing knowledge.

It's what our Týr—the one in God of War's version of Norse mythology—stood for. On my best days, I hope I do too.

I also believe one of the best ways to get a sense of a place and people is to experience their cuisine—something I imagine Týr did in every place he visited. It's a way we can step back in time, living as he would.

Now Týr, as a god with mythological means of travel at his disposal, could visit a culture, spend time with its people, breaking bread, and soaking it in. For many of us today (and for many different reasons), traveling to far-flung places isn't quite so easy. But through a culture's unique cuisine, it's still possible to feel transported.

It's something my son and I strived for not so long ago. One of his weekly school assignments centered around learning about other cultures—some ancient; some modern—but he was hungry to learn more. We'd start by getting out our small cork globe. I'd give it a spin and my son would stop it when the time was right. Then it was research time. We'd open a web browser and learn about the country under my son's small fingertip—its geography, history, music, art, and of course, its food.

This quickly led to both of us deciding on a dish we'd love to try . . . and the beauty of living in a multicultural melting pot like Los Angeles is that a restaurant with that dish was always just a short drive away. We'd walk into a local Cuban restaurant, catch a big smile from the old host wearing a spotless white guayabera shirt, and take in the wafting smell of garlic. We'd bob to the rumba music playing from tinny speakers in the drop ceiling as we shared crisp papas rellenas until the ropa vieja and lechon asado we ordered hit our table. Halfway through this incredible meal, we were transported.

In the weeks and months that followed, we visited several cultures through their food: bratwurst sitting at long oak tables, tonkotsu ramen as pretty as the photo on the menu board, perfectly cheesy pupusas, tandoori chicken, beef bulgogi—absorbing as much culture as we could through our American taste buds. Each experience led, I hope, to a broader understanding of the people providing us the wonderful gift of their heritage. It also gave my son the joy of being able to push a tiny red pin into our little globe, making him feel part of a larger world.

Then 2020 happened.

Restaurants closed for a while, and when they could finally reopen, it was only for delivery. It wouldn't be the same, but since we weren't ready to stop our cultural food adventures, we shifted to the occasional curbside take-out or tried making them as authentically as we could ourselves. We traveled to Poland for buttery pierogies. We watched flyovers of Kīlauea's lava flow while downing heaps of kalua pork. I broke out my long-ago seasoned, but heavily underused, wok to make traditional egg fried rice, and followed it up the next week with gnocchi, then jambalaya, and finally, my father's own recipe for spanakopita.

But all journeys come to an end. Eventually, we settled into new routines. With school and work under the same roof for much longer than we ever anticipated, my son defaulted back to lunch PB&Js and cheese quesadillas. I defaulted back to quick standbys too but look back to that time fondly with gratitude for the small peek into cultures we don't have god-like means of visiting.

I guess my hope is that this book, with recipes from places Týr visited, will transport you and your family for a moment in time—like my son and I felt in that Cuban restaurant. I hope you can use them to broaden your cultural perspectives, stoke a sense of adventure, and maybe, as our Norse god of war would encourage, provide you a little culinary knowledge worth sharing.

—Matt Sophos, Narrative Director, God of War Ragnarök

THE GUIDING LIGHT

Eons ago, my Aesir brethren—well, All-Father Odin primarily, but it was a consensus decision—assigned me a very distinct role in Asgardian affairs. Just like that, I became Týr, God of War. It was an odd assignment, because unlike most of my barbaric kin, I'm not fond of fighting, or killing, or debauchery. But I decided that if "war god" was to be my godly role, I'd make the most of it. Make it my own, as it were.

Over time, I quietly wove auxiliary functions into my job. I became Týr, God of Diplomacy; Týr, God of Treaties; Týr, God of Law and Justice. Thus, in a broader sense, I took on the mantle of worldy peacemaker. I also invested much in the cross-pollination of cultures—a process that can neutralize ignorance and fear of "the other" that so often leads to war between disparate lands.

In the process, I became quite fond of travel. I supped with many who would become trusted emissaries and friends.

As you might imagine, my interpretation of the war god's official duties was not always well-received by my Aesir kin.

Some expressed preference for a more warlike god—maybe a raging, red-eyed killer who lays waste to regions. Someone who loves carnage . . . like, say, Thor. Or the cruel God of War myths I'd heard in my sojourns across Midgard—the bloodthirsty destroyer-god of the Maya, or the Nubian war goddess known as "she who massacres," or perhaps the pitiless Ares of Olympus. Once, riding an imperial barge on the Yellow River, I listened to Chinese storytellers chant tales of their brutal executioner god. Apparently, the very sight of his green robes caused foes to weep and evacuate themselves. I silently considered how deeply the Aesir would adore such a god.

So, yes, my own people wanted a God of War who was more warlike. But that is not me. I'll never forget my first visit to the great city on Midgard's southern river delta. I went there seeking to secure trade routes and expand cultural exchanges—two activities that always foster better relations amongst realms. As my chariot rolled into the central palace district, I beheld the city's legendary "pensile paradise," the Hanging Gardens.

There, on terraces—a hundred feet high and literally spilling over with boughs of exotic growth irrigated by wondrous water-screw pumps—people of all races mingled in peace and the spirit of mutuality.

Observing this, one thing that struck me in particular was that communal bonds were formed by simply sharing a meal.

I see it as a verity now, even today in these dark times: Cooking, serving, and eating food together are inherently integrative activities. Communal dining invites individuals to cast aside differences. It seems to bring out the best in people. Yes, even Aesir gods.

No single tome could do justice to the bounty of delectable dishes I've sampled in my sojourns through the realms. I ate with kings and queens in the gilded halls of great civilizations. I shared food with brutal warriors and fierce horsemen. Even the most warlike amongst them dined with good humor and communal vigor.

So, then . . . I hope this adequately explains why a Norse God of War is writing a book of recipes.

Here's hoping these recipes, culled from the cornucopias of the Nine Realms and beyond, can bring you some small measure of warmth and good cheer on a frigid Fimbulwinter night.

INGREDIENTS GUIDE

COTIJA is a hard, crumbly cheese used in Mexican cuisine. The cheese is traditionally aged, which gives it a salty flavor. If cotija is difficult to find, it can be substituted with feta cheese. Cotija can be stored in the refrigerator.

FISH SAUCE is a sweet, salty, pungent liquid that is made from fermented anchovies and salt. Because its salt content is pretty high, it can be used as a salt substitute to add an extra layer of umami. Be careful to not add too much of this product because it can easily overpower a dish. Fish sauce can be stored in the pantry for 2 to 3 years.

HONEYCOMB is a natural product made by honeybees where they keep their honey. It can be stored in the pantry in an airtight container indefinitely.

KOREAN PEAR, sometimes called Asian pear, is a large pear with brown speckled skin that grows in East Asia. Korean pear is used in Korean barbecue marinades for its sweetness and to help tenderize meat. If Korean pear is difficult to find, it can be substituted with kiwi for tenderizing purposes. Bosc pears can be used for a similar taste, but not to tenderize meat. Korean pears can be stored at room temperature for about a week or in a refrigerator for several months.

MISO is a Japanese paste made from fermented soybeans. Miso comes in several varieties including white (the mildest flavor) and red (aged for longer, giving it a saltier and stronger flavor). Miso can be stored in an airtight container in the refrigerator.

TAHINI is a paste made from ground white sesame seeds and oil. Store-bought tahini can be stored in the pantry for up to 6 months.

TARO is a root vegetable and plant found in South Asia. It is important to note that raw taro is toxic to consume due to high levels of calcium oxalate. The outside skin should be removed before cooking. Gloves are recommended when working with raw taro in order to avoid skin irritation.

TONKATSU SAUCE is a thick, sweet sauce used in Japanese cuisine. Once opened, it must be stored in the refrigerator in an airtight container for up to 2 months.

DIETARY RESTRICTIONS

I find cooking to be a very creative hobby. It brings our friends and family together to set aside our differences and enjoy a hearty meal. You'll want to make sure to keep in mind any dietary restrictions when working your way through these recipes. Many of them can be easily adjusted to accommodate your needs. Remember, with cooking you can be innovative!

ADAPTING TO VEGETARIAN DIETS

Several recipes in this book are vegetarian or vegan. Many other recipes can be adapted to your dietary needs. Replace meat broth with vegetable broth. Swap out proteins with your favorite grilled vegetable or meat substitute. This can affect the cooking times, so plan ahead.

ADAPTING TO GLUTEN-FREE DIETS

For most recipes, you can use equal ratios of gluten substitute for flour, but be prepared to modify the quantity just in case it alters the consistency.

ADAPTING TO LACTOSE-FREE DIETS

Replace milk and heavy cream with your favorite non-dairy milk. There are also plenty of butter alternatives that I would highly recommend in place of butter. I don't suggest replacing butter with oil because it doesn't give the same consistency needed for certain recipes. If you do use oil instead, add it in small batches to see how it affects the consistency.

A REALM BETWEEN REALMS

Most sentient folk in the Northlands know that Yggdrasil, the great yew, sits at the center of the world. Yet oddly enough, almost no one knows how the World Tree's branches form pathways along the hidden seams of the Nine Realms—creating a "Realm Between Realms," as it were. Some Dwarves I've met (including the Huldra brothers) have mastered the otherworldly art of "slipping sideways" into this ethereal space. But most people, even Jötunn seers and seiðr practitioners, are entirely unaware of Yggdrasil's strange connective network.

Long ago, I devised a magical stone that gave me unfettered access to the Realm Between Realms, and thus, a way to expedite my travel across and between all Nine Realms. I called it the Unity Stone; I fancied it a conduit between cultures that would foster peace, understanding, and good will.

For many years, I used this Unity Stone for fast travel between or within our Norse realms. My trips were typically of high purpose; I might rush between clans to broker a cessation of hostilities, or ratify a treaty. But sometimes the trip was what I'd call a "spice dash." I'd be planning a diplomatic banquet and suddenly realize I needed a native seasoning, stock, or herb—a special taste from the home realm of a delegation. I wanted the food to honor every culture at the table.

Into the Realm Between Realms I'd go, dashing to another gateway to procure an ingredient for a spice mix with local flavors.

That's why I list my favorite inter-realm seasonings in this section. The Realm Between Realms was often a godsend for my cooking.

One other thing about the Realm Between Realms must be said. Earlier, I mentioned the general ignorance of Yggdrasil's hidden pathways. As it turns out, that ignorance helped protect the Jötnar from genocide.

The Jötnar had long avoided a direct conflict with Asgard by maintaining peaceful relations with the neighboring realms through goodwill and trade. But once Thor acquired his mighty hammer Mjölnir, the tide turned quickly. Forced to retreat to their homeland, the Giants asked for my help in sealing off their realm— after all, it was my own Temple that so easily facilitated inter-realm travel. I rushed secretly to Jötunheim, met with the Jötnar, and together we formulated a plan.

First off, we needed to remove the Jötunheim travel tower from the Lake of Nine shore in Midgard. Hiding an entire tower, as you might suspect, is no easy feat. It required a clever combination of subterfuge, mechanical savvy, and brute strength. Fortunately, Giants were master builders, and many, like the legendary stonemason Thamur, were also quite massive and powerful. Moving the Jötunheim tower proved surprisingly easy. But we needed a secret place to stash it! And that's when I thought of the Realm Between Realms.

It was tricky, but I devised a way to slip the structure into the hidden realm. Then, for added security, we concocted an elaborate arrangement to hide the Unity Stone, using an almost amusingly complex set of mechanisms and puzzles that required severing massive chains and flipping an entire temple upside-down!

Thus, the shadowy realm's remoteness served a great purpose. Or so we thought at the time.

JÖTUNN SPICE MIXTURE

D id you know that certain seeds can be ground into a fine powder that bestows a remarkable flavor to foods? Here's one of my favorite seasonings, passed on from a northlands Jötunn clan I met on a wintry trek many years ago. To season a deep iron crock of venison stew, the Giants put caraway and fennel seeds through a fine grinder, added a few other basic herbs, and coated the meat before cooking. The result was an astoundingly delicious meal, one that served as a warm, comforting counterpoint to the desolate windswept highlands where I hiked in search of reclusive stonemasons for my temple-building project on Midgard's Lake of Nine.

DIFFICULTY: Easy

PREP TIME: 5 minutes

YIELD: ⅔ cup

DIETARY NOTES: Dairy-Free, Vegan

INGREDIENTS:

2 teaspoons (8 grams) caraway seeds

2 teaspoons (6 grams) fennel seeds

2 teaspoons (2 grams) dried thyme

2 tablespoons (6 grams) dried dill weed

3 tablespoons (5 grams) dried tarragon

1 tablespoon (11 grams) onion powder

Place the caraway and fennel seeds in a spice grinder and blend until finely ground. Transfer to an airtight container and combine with the thyme, dill, tarragon, and onion powder. Can be stored at room temperature for up to 3 months.

DWARVEN SPICE MIXTURE

◆

The Dwarves love this delectable spice rub that toasts nuts and seeds then crushes them into a salty grind. Rubbed on a leg of lamb, the seasoning transforms merely good meat into something transcendent. I was fortunate to have smuggled this recipe out of Svartalfheim before the vindictive All-Father used his magicks to slam its gates shut!

DIFFICULTY: Easy

PREP TIME: 15 minutes

COOK TIME: 10 minutes

YIELD: 1 cup

DIETARY NOTES: Dairy-Free, Vegan

◇

INGREDIENTS:

⅓ cup (56 grams) hazelnuts

3 tablespoons (36 grams) pistachios

2 tablespoons (29 grams) almonds

¼ cup (34 grams) sesame seeds

2 tablespoons (10 grams) coriander seeds

1 tablespoon (8 grams) cumin seeds

2 teaspoons (4 grams) fennel seeds

1 teaspoon (4 grams) salt

Preheat the oven to 350°F (177°C). Place the hazelnuts, pistachios, and almonds on a baking sheet and bake until slightly toasted, about 8 to 10 minutes. Let cool slightly, then transfer to a grinder. Grind until coarsely ground. Transfer to an airtight container.

Heat a medium nonstick pan over medium heat. Add all of the seeds. Constantly move the pan until all sides of the seeds are toasted, about 4 minutes.

Transfer to a spice grinder and grind until coarsely ground. Pour into the container with the nuts. Add the salt and mix together. Can be stored at room temperature for up to 1 month.

SPARTAN SPICE MIXTURE

◆

Kratos is a true Spartan in his simple, stripped-down tastes. But I was surprised—more like shocked, to be honest—when one night he offered to prepare a meal, then proceeded to whip up . . . a mushroom quiche! Kratos and quiche? It seemed an unlikely combination. Yet something he did gave that pie an exotic flavor and character that I found quite remarkable.

Kratos was clearly unamused by my delight, and when I asked him the secret ingredient, he said, "Pepper." But after days of harassment, I finally got him to divulge his Spartan spice mix recipe. Nothing fancy here, the simplest of ingredients . . . but, as Kratos explained later, the true secret is to maintain the delicate balance of so many wonderful herbs and powders. "How much, matters," he said. Quite an insight from such a hulking, brutish man.

DIFFICULTY: Easy
PREP TIME: 5 minutes
YIELD: ⅔ cup
DIETARY NOTES: Dairy-Free, Vegan

◆

INGREDIENTS:

1 tablespoon (10 grams) garlic powder

½ tablespoon (5 grams) onion powder

1 tablespoon (2 grams) dried basil

1 teaspoon (1 gram) dried thyme

1½ tablespoons (3 grams) dried Greek oregano

½ tablespoon (2 grams) dried marjoram

1 teaspoon (1 gram) dried parsley

¼ teaspoon (1 gram) ground cinnamon

1 teaspoon (1 gram) dried rosemary

1 teaspoon (2 grams) black pepper

2 teaspoons (8 grams) salt

Combine all ingredients in an airtight container. Store at room temperature for up to 3 months.

CHINESE FIVE-SPICE MIXTURE

◆

This seasoning mix is truly one of the wonders of the cosmos. If you think that's hyperbole, you clearly haven't had a salmon banh mi that was marinated overnight in Chinese five-spice. Cooking based on Chinese methods has permeated the realms, and Chinese five-spice has worked its way into recipes well beyond Midgard's eastern reaches, including even Asgard. The melding of its five perfectly balanced and complementary flavors—fennel, cinnamon, cloves, Szechuan peppercorns, and star anise— seems like something that must have emerged whole and entirely essential from the great void of Ginnungagap.

DIFFICULTY: Easy

PREP TIME: 10 minutes

YIELD: ⅔ cup

DIETARY NOTES: Dairy-Free, Vegan

◇

INGREDIENTS:

1 cinnamon stick

1 tablespoon (3 grams) Szechuan peppercorns

1½ tablespoons (8 grams) fennel seeds

10 whole cloves

5 star anise pods

Place all ingredients in a spice grinder and blend until the peppercorns are ground. Place in an airtight container. Can be stored at room temperature for up to 3 months.

CURRY SPICE MIXTURE

◆

It's hard to believe that something this flavorful with such a long list of ingredients can be so easy to make. That you can mix up a batch of curry spice in 10 minutes is a real blessing in a pinch, let me tell you. For example, if an unexpected visitor drops in—say, a Valkyrie queen—you can use it to dress up plain carrots or a pork tenderloin, turning them into banquet-quality servings.

Yes, I received a few surprise visits from Freya, back when we were both still royalty in the Asgardian court. This impressive, powerful woman came to me seeking advice regarding Odin's increasingly mercurial temperament. I was humbled by her presumption of my wisdom, but I fear I let her down. My abiding faith in reasonable solutions and fair outcomes . . . in the cosmic arc of justice, and in the fundamental goodness of Gods and Mortals . . . all of this made me too optimistic by half. It colored my judgment. It shaded the advice I gave my esteemed visitor.

Ah, well. At least I gave her good food, well-seasoned.

DIFFICULTY: Easy

PREP TIME: 10 minutes

YIELD: 1 cup

DIETARY NOTES: Dairy-Free, Vegan

◇

INGREDIENTS:

3 tablespoons (10 grams) coriander seeds

1½ tablespoons (13 grams) cumin seeds

1 tablespoon (5 grams) fennel seeds

6 black peppercorns

1 star anise pod

3 whole cloves

3 green cardamom pods

2 black cardamom pods

½ cinnamon stick

1 teaspoon (8 grams) ground fenugreek seeds

½ teaspoon ground nutmeg

1 teaspoon (2 grams) ground allspice

1 teaspoon (2 grams) ground ginger powder

1½ tablespoons (10 grams) ground turmeric

2 to 3 teaspoons (6 to 9 grams) Kashmiri chili powder

Place the coriander seeds, cumin seeds, fennel seeds, peppercorns, star anise, cloves, green and black cardamom, and cinnamon stick in a spice grinder and blend until ground. Place in an airtight container and combine with the remaining spices and Kashmiri chili powder to taste. Can be stored at room temperature for up to 3 months.

MIDGARD

Midgard truly fascinates me. Easily the most multifarious of the nine realms, this world crafted by primordial gods for Mortals features a teeming diversity of habitat and culture not seen in other realms.

In the old days, before my lost years and Fimbulwinter, every trip I made across the so-called "middle world" seemed to reveal things unexpected and often delightful. Even though Midgard is the realm of human mortals, its centrality on Yggdrasil's branches has opened its lands to outsiders in ways that other realms do not.

This is particularly true in the realm's northlands. Up north, the River Pass once served as a bustling trade route lined with crowded marketplaces that drew all races, even gods. Dwarves from Svartalfheim tapped the precious metals from the mines of Völunder and Landsuther, and built imposing strongholds at Veithurgard and Konùnsgard. The great caverns inside Midgard's towering Mountain became a haven for Giants, who mined its ores and gave shelter to artists and other outcasts. Even the Valkyries of Valhalla built a secret council chamber on Midgard's Lake of Nine shore.

Thus, it made sense to focus my vision here, to build a travel hub at the center of the great World Tree. It would offer quick, easy passage between realms from this middle world where Mortals, Elves, Dwarves, Giants, and even Gods have been known to trade goods, break bread together, and hoist tankards of ale with toasts and lusty cheers.

Raising the Temple of Týr and installing its realm travel room was a great triumph— not for me, but for all peace-loving folk in all realms. At least, that's what I believed.

The Midgard recipes I share all come from a particular feast I hosted long ago. That banquet, held in the central hall of my temple on Midgard's Lake of Nine, turned out to be my last good banquet for quite a while.

Some years after the union of Freya with Odin had finalized a triumphant truce between Aesir and Vanir, all realms enjoyed an interval of peace marked by the birth of the couple's son, Baldur. But Odin's paranoid focus on prophecy began to fester again. His eagerness to learn and experiment with Freya's magic had dark purposes, as we all soon discovered.

Odin also began to suspect (correctly, of course) that his own God of War, Týr, had maneuvered behind his back to help the Vanir in their own fights against the Aesir. Rumors were spreading that Freya's brother, Freyr, was unhappy with the union and planning something. The All-Father also resented all the loving attention I was getting across the realms. People of all races, it turns out, love peacemakers.

Thus, that "feast" in my hall sought to address these issues. Over platters of roast quail in my brand new temple, I implored the guests to be ready for anything. I knew the All-Father and he had some sort of plan. I warned the other attendees, all emissaries from other realms, that a new Aesir offensive against their lands seemed inevitable. Unity and resolve would be important.

"I hate war," I told them. "But we must be ready."

As my staff served mulled apple juice, goat cheese, and apple tarts to the guests, we had a meal unlikely to be seen over the centuries to come. People from all the realms shared food and drink in a celebration that Odin would make impossible in his mad search for knowledge. We even had displays of genius by those mad Huldra brothers, making delicacies of ice confection that delighted even the sourest of disposition.

That meal became the last true pleasure I had before the All-Father brought ruin into the realms. There was little to celebrate until I ended up in a dank, darkened cell and became the subject of daily torture, ruthlessly administered by the All-Father himself. While I was in that cell, I choked down daily rations of moldy bread and gruel. Every feeding—and these were indeed "feedings," not meals—I closed my eyes and saw that feast, its heaping plate of pork tenderloin with rødkål and hasselbackpoteter on the side.

I'm convinced my food fantasies kept me sane and alive. And even though I'm not yet fully convinced it was *worth* it to survive, I have to say . . . cooking and eating a good meal always helps stoke the fires of hope!

ROAST QUAIL

The realm of Midgard is a hunter's paradise—or was, until Fimbulwinter drove much of the wildlife into extended hibernation. Wild game was so abundant in days past that the Mortals of Midgard often invited other races to hunt here. Wild animals, fowl, and fish of every stripe thrived in this realm's ecosystems and made for some fine eating. Quail has long been a particular favorite of mine, and I learned this easy sear-and-roast recipe from a food vendor in the seaside village of Njörðholm. Years ago, that town was a delightful place to visit. However, one fateful day, it became a chilly nexus of conflict between Aesir, Vanir, and Jötnar . . . with its poor human inhabitants suffering the fallout. Today, Njörðholm lies under a crust of ice that actually pre-dates the advent of Fimbulwinter.

The town's sad tale begins brightly enough, with a clan of fishers so fond of the Vanir god Njörð that they named their town after him. Njörð loved to visit the village, feast on fish and quail in the local jarl's great banquet hall, and drink himself silly. He liked the place so much that he'd spin seiðr magics to calm the wind and seas for the Njörðholm fishing fleet.

But one day, the Jötunn stonemason Thamur was passing Njörðholm when Thor caught up with him and hammered the massive Frost Giant's chisel right through his head. The mountainous Thamur's fall crushed the town . . . and his dying breath was so bitterly frigid that it froze Njörðholm and the landscape for miles around. Today, the town is nothing but a haven for Draugr, Wulvers, and Ogres. Some of the finest quail hunting grounds in Midgard now lie buried under an icy crust.

DIFFICULTY: Easy

PREP TIME: 10 minutes

COOK TIME: 20 minutes

YIELD: 4 servings

DIETARY NOTES: Dairy-Free, Gluten-Free

INGREDIENTS:

4 whole quails

Salt

Black pepper

2 rosemary sprigs, halved

2 tablespoons (26 grams) olive oil

1 tablespoon (21 grams) honey

2 cloves garlic, minced

1 teaspoon (2 grams) ground fennel

Preheat the oven to 425°F (218°C). Generously salt and pepper the quails. Place a half sprig of rosemary in the cavity of each quail. Combine the olive oil, honey, garlic, and fennel in a small bowl. Brush it onto each quail.

Heat a medium cast-iron skillet over medium-high heat. Sear all sides of the quails until golden brown, about 4 to 5 minutes.

Transfer to the oven and cook for 10 minutes, or until they reach an internal temperature of 165°F (74°C) on an instant-read thermometer.

PORK TENDERLOIN

ere's another tried-and-true Midgard delicacy: a solid pound of pork tenderloin rubbed in spices, garlic, and olive oil before being wrapped in prosciutto, seared in cast iron, and oven-baked. I'm somewhat loathe to admit that I learned this recipe from a northland wilderness clan of men who called themselves Reavers. Back then, Reavers hunted Midgard's wild boar with a relentless passion. Afterward, their preparation of the tenderloin cut was as precise as a holy ritual.

DIFFICULTY: Medium

PREP TIME: 35 minutes

COOK TIME: 20 minutes, plus 40 minutes to rest

YIELD: 4 servings

DIETARY NOTES: Dairy-Free, Gluten-Free

INGREDIENTS:

6 cloves garlic, minced

2 tablespoons (26 grams) olive oil

2½ tablespoons (11 grams) Jötunn Spice Mixture (page 15)

2 teaspoons (5 grams) Curry Spice Mixture (page 23)

1½ teaspoons (3 grams) ground fennel

1 pound (454 grams) pork tenderloin

5 ounces (142 grams) sliced prosciutto

Combine the garlic, olive oil, Jötunn and Curry spices, and ground fennel in a small bowl. Cut a slit in the length of the pork tenderloin, making sure not to cut all the way through, leaving the ends sealed. Open the tenderloin and rub the oil mixture over all parts of it. Fill the cut section with the remaining oil mixture. Pinch the tenderloin closed. Wrap it with prosciutto until it is fully covered. Wrap in plastic wrap and refrigerate for 30 minutes.

Preheat the oven to 425°F (218°C). Heat a large cast-iron skillet over medium-high heat. Remove the plastic wrap from the tenderloin and sear each side of the pork, about 2 minutes per side.

Transfer the tenderloin to the oven and cook for 10 minutes, or until it reaches an internal temperature of 145°F (63°C) on an instant-read thermometer. Remove, cover with aluminum foil, and let rest for 10 minutes before slicing.

HASSELBACKPOTETER

I mentioned previously how images of this twice-buttered russet potato dish helped keep me alive and somewhat sane during the interminable decades of my incarceration by the All-Father. Who would think that a recipe so simple could imprint itself so deeply in one's gastronomic memory?

DIFFICULTY: Easy

PREP TIME: 20 minutes

COOK TIME: 1 hour

YIELD: 3 servings

DIETARY NOTES: Vegetarian, Gluten-Free

INGREDIENTS:

5 tablespoons (70 grams) unsalted butter, melted

2 tablespoons (26 grams) olive oil

1 tablespoon (5 grams) Jötunn Spice Mixture (page 15)

1 teaspoon (4 grams) garlic powder

3 large russet potatoes

Fresh chives, minced, for serving

Preheat the oven to 425°F (218°C). Combine the butter, olive oil, Jötunn Spice Mixture, and garlic powder in a small bowl. Slice the potatoes thinly, but don't cut all the way through.

Place the potatoes on a baking sheet and brush them on top and between the slices with half of the butter mixture. Bake for 30 minutes. Remove the potatoes, brush them with the remaining butter mixture, and bake for another 30 minutes, or until tender. Serve with chives.

RØDKÅL

I first sampled this sweet and sour cabbage dish at a campsite in the rugged Midgard Foothills, deep in the late-day shadow of the Mountain. For years, the Foothills region served as a staging ground for the mining operations inside Midgard's great peak. Adventurers often pitched their base camps in these hills, too, seeking to scale the Mountain, a most difficult endeavor. Some said dragons guarded the summit pass, a place shrouded in mystery, and nearly impossible to reach. At night I would sit by the fire with a stone bowl of rødkål in one hand and a mug of sack mead in the other, listening to rollicking tales of crazy adventurers riding Ogres and killing Trolls.

DIFFICULTY: Easy

PREP TIME: 15 minutes

COOK TIME: 1 hour

YIELD: 6 to 8 servings

DIETARY NOTES: Vegan, Gluten-Free, Dairy-free

INGREDIENTS:

2 tablespoons (26 grams) olive oil

1 large red cabbage, cored and thinly sliced

⅔ cup (150 grams) cherry juice

⅓ cup (75 grams) apple cider vinegar

2 tablespoons (30 grams) sugar

1 teaspoon (3 grams) salt, plus more to taste

Black pepper

Heat the olive oil in a deep pot over medium-high heat. Add the cabbage, stir, and cook for 5 minutes. Add the cherry juice, apple cider vinegar, sugar, and salt. Bring to a light boil and then reduce the heat to medium-low. Cover and cook until the cabbage is tender, about 45 minutes. Season with additional salt and pepper. Serve warm or refrigerate to serve cold.

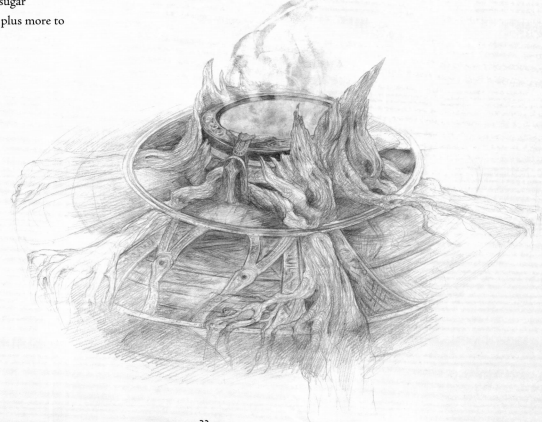

MUSHROOM QUICHE

I mentioned earlier that Kratos, of all people, makes a killer mushroom quiche. When the big brute holds leeks in his enormous hand, they look like blades of grass. Yet, his patience and skill with the recipe's delicate steps truly impressed me. His demeanor was changed—cooking seemed like a meditation, and as the hearth fire glinted in his eye, I began to suspect that quiche-making placed his heart in touch with someone for whom he once cooked regularly.

DIFFICULTY: Medium

PREP TIME: 45 minutes, plus at least 10 minutes to cool

COOK TIME: 1 hour 20 minutes

YIELD: 8 servings

DIETARY NOTES: Vegetarian

INGREDIENTS:

1 tablespoon (13 grams) olive oil

2 leeks, white and light green parts only, thinly sliced

1 pound (454 grams) white mushrooms, stemmed and sliced

4 ounces (113 grams) shiitake mushrooms, stemmed and sliced

6 eggs

½ teaspoon (2 grams) salt

½ teaspoon (1 gram) black pepper

2 teaspoons (4 grams) Spartan Spice Mixture (page 19)

1 cup (242 grams) half-and-half

¼ cup (56 grams) butter, melted

Fifteen 9-by-14-inch (23-by-36-centimeter) phyllo dough sheets, defrosted

4 ounces (113 grams) Gruyère cheese, shredded

Heat a medium frying pan with 1 teaspoon olive oil over medium-high heat. Add the leeks and cook until just crisped, about 4 minutes. Transfer to a plate. Add the remaining olive oil to the pan and sauté the mushrooms. Cook until the mushrooms have softened and crisped slightly, about 10 minutes. Transfer to the plate with the leeks. Set aside.

Whisk together the eggs, salt, pepper, Spartan Spice Mixture, and half-and-half until well combined. Set aside.

Preheat the oven to 350°F (177°C). Prepare a 9-inch (23-centimeter) cake pan by brushing it with some of the melted butter. Place a sheet of phyllo dough in the pan. Brush with butter and top with another sheet of phyllo dough. Repeat with all of the phyllo sheets.

Place the Gruyère cheese on top of the layered phyllo dough. Top with the sautéed mushrooms and leeks. Carefully pour the egg mixture on top. If the phyllo dough is taller than the filling, lightly press it down until it's just taller or level with the filling. Bake for 50 to 60 minutes, or until set. Transfer it to a cooling rack and let cool for at least 10 minutes before cutting and serving.

MAKE SURE THAT THE PHYLLO SHEETS EVENLY COVER THE SIDES OF THE PAN. YOU DON'T WANT ANY SECTION OF YOUR QUICHE'S CRUST TO BE TOO THIN.

PHYLLO DOUGH IS EXTREMELY DELICATE, SO BE GENTLE WITH EACH SHEET! KEEP THE SHEETS COVERED WITH A KITCHEN TOWEL WHEN YOU AREN'T WORKING WITH THEM. THEY DRY VERY EASILY.

GOAT CHEESE AND APPLE TARTS

This elegant pastry requires a light touch. Oddly enough, I'm told the recipe originated with the Giants Meløða and Qnþreis, founders of the Jötunn haven in the huge central caverns of Midgard's Mountain. From there, it got passed on to Dwarves then filtered out into the human settlements in the region. The Mountain's Jötunn community began as a shelter for artists, and flourished for many decades . . . until the carnage wrought by Thor and Mjölnir drove all Giants back to Jötunheim. A clan of Dwarves moved in next and mined ore in the caverns. Eventually a few Trolls, a monstrous Ancient, lots of Draugr, and the fearsome dragon Hræzlyr chased out the Dwarves too. Somehow, the recipe for goat cheese and apple tarts survived all this tumult and transition.

DIFFICULTY: Medium

PREP TIME: 30 minutes

COOK TIME: 30 minutes

YIELD: 8 servings

DIETARY NOTES: Vegetarian

INGREDIENTS:

8 ounces (228 grams) goat cheese

2 tablespoons (30 grams) ricotta cheese

3 tablespoons (52 grams) apple juice, plus more if needed

2 tablespoons (28 grams) lemon juice

¼ cup (84 grams) plus 3 tablespoons (63 grams) honey

1 teaspoon (4 grams) vanilla extract

½ teaspoon (3 grams) salt

2 puff pastry sheets, defrosted

2 tablespoons (28 grams) butter, melted

2 Gala apples, peeled, cored, and thinly sliced

Ground cardamom, for topping

Combine the goat cheese, ricotta cheese, apple juice, lemon juice, 3 tablespoons (63 grams) honey, vanilla extract, and salt in a medium bowl. Mix until smooth. If the mixture is too thick and clumpy, add more apple juice.

Preheat the oven to 375°F (191°C). Cut the puff pastry sheets into 5-inch (13-centimeter) circles, four per sheet. Take a 3-inch (7½-centimeter) cookie cutter and lightly press in the center of each of the rounds, but do not cut all the way through. Transfer to a baking sheet lined with parchment paper. Using a spatula or large spoon, spread the goat cheese filling over each tart, keeping it within the indent.

Combine the butter and ¼ cup (84 grams) honey in a small bowl. Top each tart with apple slices (about ¼ of an apple). Brush each tart with the butter honey mixture and sprinkle with cardamom. Bake for 25 to 30 minutes. Serve warm or at room temperature.

MULLED APPLE JUICE

This hot drink, so easy to make, was hoisted in toast at many a winter's treaty ceremony. Just toss it all together in a cauldron and whisk a bit as you heat it up. Once, in northern Midgard, I mediated a dispute between two angry Norse retinues who both claimed ownership of a worthless strip of ice jutting between their kingdoms. That night, a monstrous blizzard nearly buried the longhouse where we met. As it turned out, we got snowed in for three days.

By day two, the sides began sharing food as we collected enough scraps for decent meals. That evening we ran out of mead, and switched to my mulled apple juice. As its cinnamon citrus aroma wafted like a narcotic through the great room, I let it work its magic. By the time we finally managed to burrow out to clear the main road, the two jarls had signed an agreement to share the ridiculous frozen isthmus. Neither would leave without my apple juice recipe.

DIFFICULTY: Easy

PREP TIME: 5 minutes

COOK TIME: 20 minutes

YIELD: 4 servings

DIETARY NOTES: Vegetarian, Gluten-Free

INGREDIENTS:

4 cups (946 milliliters) apple juice

1 cinnamon stick

4 cardamom pods

6 whole cloves

1 orange, sliced

1 lemon, sliced

2-inch (5-centimeter) piece of ginger, grated

3 tablespoons (63 grams) honey

Place all of the ingredients in a medium pot over medium-high heat. Whisk until the honey has dissolved. Bring to a boil. Reduce heat to low and simmer for 15 minutes. Serve hot.

ALFHEIM

Every realm is impressive in its own right. . . yes, even Helheim has certain charms. But the Elven realm shimmers with beauty of another spectrum. Its waterways, woods, and even barrens seem to glisten as if infused with the great Light of Alfheim itself. And nowhere in my travels have I seen an edifice more majestic than the great Ringed Temple of the Light Elves, an architectural wonder of the first rank. Freyr himself directed its construction—in fact, Mimir often refers to it as "Freyr's Temple."

When in Alfheim, though, one must remember: The realm is not all "light." Indeed, equally magnificent structures exist underground, the amorphous hive of chambers and passages where dwell the Dark Elves. It is a shadowy reflection of the citadel above. Both are equally remarkable, as are the people themselves.

For this reason, it saddens me to learn of the ongoing warfare between the two factions. According to Mimir, the savagery of their strife has rivaled that of the worst Aesir thuggery. Before my imprisonment, the Dark and Light cousins lived in peace—an uneasy peace, but peace nonetheless. Back then, their deep respect for the Vanir lord Freyr—one of the few gods ever allowed into Alfheim— kept both sides in line. But I'm told that in subsequent years, the accord failed and nothing could blunt their internecine fury. Even today, with Ragnarök behind us, renegade clans of both Elven races refuse to give up the feud.

This thought brings to mind a visit I once made to Alfheim, long ago.

I went seeking pledges from both Light and Dark Elves to join all other races—Gods, Giants, Dwarves, and Mortals—in building a great hub for inter-realm travel. My plan was to construct this hub in the most central realm, Midgard, right in the middle of the Lake of Nine.

I approached the Light Elves first, and after a full day of feasting and talk, I left the Ringed Temple's great hall with a firm guarantee of cooperation from the Light Council. The Light Elves also warned me that their dark insectile kin in Alfheim's subterranean hives might impede the general agreement.

In those days, I believed in the power of diplomacy; I felt I could broker a deal with anybody. I had great faith in the fundamental commonality of all races. After all, we come from the same roots, literally—the roots of Yggdrasil. More specific to Alfheim, Freyr's calm influence was still strong in that realm. So, the next day, I left the Ringed Temple, crossed the stark blue-sand desert to the north, and descended directly into the governing commune of the Dark Elves.

It was indeed a shadowy place, but the Dark Elf leader, Svartáljǫfurr, emerged from his warren and greeted me most humbly. With a gesture, he ordered up a feast no less sumptuous than the one I'd enjoyed the day before. Elven dishes, Dark or Light, are prepared with exquisite care and served with gracious good humor and a spirit of sharing.

Hours later, as we worked out the final details of Svartáljǫfurr's generous commitment of resources to my realm-travel

project, I found myself strangely comforted by the dark, organic luminescence of his council chamber. As if reading my thoughts, Svartáljǫfurr leaned in and asked if I'd enjoyed my Alfheim visit. I said I had indeed, from start to finish.

Then he told me something Freyr once told me, something I'll never forget: "Neither light nor darkness is inherently good or bad. One can be blinded by either quality, as easily as by prejudice. Lord Freyr knew this well, and that's why he will be ever beloved by all Elves."

BEET TERRINE

When I was younger, I didn't like beets. I didn't realize how a properly prepared beet dish like this Elven terrine can be such a culinary masterpiece. It takes some hard work, but the final product is worthy of the full glow of the Light of Alfheim.

DIFFICULTY: Hard

PREP TIME: 45 minutes, plus 12 hours to chill

COOK TIME: 45 minutes

YIELD: 8 servings

DIETARY NOTES: Vegetarian

INGREDIENTS:

8 ounces (227 grams) golden beets, tops removed

1 pound (454 grams) red beets, tops removed

GOAT CHEESE FILLING:

16 ounces (454 grams) goat cheese

4 cloves garlic, finely minced

2 tablespoons plus 1 teaspoon (7 grams) fresh chives

2 teaspoons (4 grams) lemon zest

1 teaspoon (2 grams) orange zest

2 teaspoons (10 grams) lemon juice

2 teaspoons (10 grams) orange juice

Arugula, for serving

✳ ✳ Place the different beets in two separate large pots with water over high heat. Bring to a boil, reduce the heat to medium, and simmer until the beets are tender all the way through and can be pierced with a toothpick easily, 45 to 50 minutes.

To make the goat cheese filling: While the beets are cooking, combine the goat cheese, garlic, chives, lemon and orange zest, and both juices in a medium bowl. Mix until completely incorporated. Cover and refrigerate until ready to use.

Drain the beets and let cool before peeling and discarding the skin. Thinly slice the beets to ⅛ inch (3 millimeters) thick.

Prepare a 9-by-5-by-3-inch (23-by-13-by-8-centimeter) loaf pan by layering plastic wrap inside, with about 4 inches (10 centimeters) extra hanging over the edges. Place half of the sliced red beets in a layer at the bottom of the pan.

Spread half of the goat cheese filling evenly across the beets. Top with the sliced golden beets. Add the remaining goat cheese mixture and spread evenly. Finally, top with the remaining red beets.

Completely cover the beets with the extra plastic wrap, plus more if needed. Gently press down. Refrigerate for at least 12 hours before cutting and serving with arugula.

✳ ✳ MAKE SURE TO PUT THE BEETS IN TWO DIFFERENT POTS TO AVOID THE RED ONES DYEING THE GOLDEN ONES. I'D ALSO RECOMMEND WEARING PLASTIC GLOVES TO AVOID DYEING YOUR HANDS WHILE PREPARING.

MERCIMEKLI KÖFTE

This wonderful lentil ball dish is one of the best appetizer recipes I've found anywhere in the realms. This one is a Dark Elf special, served in the hive's common halls when entertaining visitors, something the dark ones rarely do, it is true. But I believe mercimekli köfte is also a regularly featured meze at all ceremonial meals in Alfheim's subterranean dwelling spaces.

DIFFICULTY: Easy

PREP TIME: 20 minutes

COOK TIME: 20 minutes, plus 3 hours 20 minutes to rest

YIELD: 6 servings

DIETARY NOTES: Vegan, Gluten-Free

IN COLLABORATION WITH:
Göksu Uğur

INGREDIENTS:

1 cup (190 grams) red lentils

2½ cups (600 milliliters) water

1 cup (200 grams) bulgur

¼ cup (52 grams) plus 1 tablespoon (13 grams) olive oil

1 medium onion, chopped

3 cloves garlic, minced

5 tablespoons (70 grams) tomato paste

2 teaspoons (7 grams) salt, plus more for seasoning

½ teaspoon (1 gram) black pepper, plus more for seasoning

2 teaspoons (6 grams) ground cumin

1 teaspoon (3 grams) ground cayenne pepper, plus more for seasoning

2 teaspoons (7 grams) fresh mint, chopped

1 cup (50 grams) fresh parsley, chopped

4 scallions, chopped

Butter lettuce, for serving

3 lemons, sliced for serving

Combine the lentils and water in a medium pot. Heat over medium heat and bring to a boil. Reduce the heat to low and simmer for 10 minutes. Remove from the heat, add the bulgur, and cover. Let sit for 15 to 20 minutes, until the bulgur is cooked through. Set aside.

Heat a medium nonstick pan with 1 tablespoon (13 grams) olive oil over medium-high heat. Add the onions and cook until softened, about 5 minutes. Add the garlic and cook until the onions begin to brown, another 3 minutes. Add the tomato paste, stir, and cook for another 2 minutes. Remove from the heat and set aside.

Transfer the lentils and bulgur to a large bowl. Add ¼ cup (52 grams) of olive oil and mix well, lightly mashing the lentils. Add the sautéed vegetables and mix together.

Add the spices, fresh mint, parsley, and scallions and mix until it just comes together. Season with additional salt, black pepper, and cayenne pepper.

Split into golf ball–sized portions and place in an airtight container. Refrigerate for at least 3 hours before serving with butter lettuce and lemons.

SPANAKOPITA

Both of Alfheim's Elven races, Dark and Light, are true connoisseurs of vegetarian cuisine. This savory spinach pie originated in Midgard's region of Greece, a place I've found to be a food lover's delight. But somehow, the recipe emigrated to Alfheim and became a favorite Light Elf dish. In fact, I first sampled spanakopita in the Ringed Temple, and I take full credit for spreading it to finer dining halls across the other realms. Every place I prepared this dish during my travels became enamored of it practically overnight. Part of its allure here in the northern lands is the association with Light Elves, whose aura of mystery and transcendence continues to enchant other cultures to this very day ... even in a world caught up in the throes of Fimbulwinter. It also happens to be amazingly delectable. Even Mimir, who hasn't eaten anything in years, says he still salivates at the smell of baking spanakopita.

DIFFICULTY: Medium

PREP TIME: 45 minutes

COOK TIME: 1 hour

YIELD: 12 servings

DIETARY NOTES: Vegetarian

IN COLLABORATION WITH:
Matt Sophos

INGREDIENTS:

2½ pounds (1,134 grams) fresh spinach, washed and drained, finely chopped

8 scallions, finely chopped

1½ pounds (680 grams) feta cheese, crumbled

4 eggs

½ pound (227 grams) salted butter, melted

Eighteen 9-by-14-inch (23-by-36-centimeter) phyllo dough sheets, defrosted

Combine the spinach, scallions, and feta cheese in a large bowl. Add the eggs and mix until fully combined.

Preheat the oven to 350°F (177°C). Prepare a 9-by-13-by-2-inch (23-by-33-by-5-centimeter) baking dish by brushing it with some of the butter. Place a phyllo dough sheet inside and brush with butter. Press another phyllo sheet into the buttered sheet and brush with butter. Repeat until there are 4 layers of phyllo dough.

Spread a third of the spinach mixture on top. Top with 4 more phyllo sheets, with butter between each. Add another third of the spinach mixture. Top with 4 more buttered phyllo sheets. Add the remaining filling. Top with phyllo sheets.

Bake for 45 to 60 minutes, until golden brown. Let cool slightly before cutting into 12 pieces.

AISH BALADI

Widely known as "Egyptian flatbread," this succulent baked good first spread into Alfheim from an extended factfinding mission I conducted in Egypt at the behest of the Dark and Light Elves. Some Elves, tired of their own racial bickering, were interested in learning how multiracial civilizations in Midgard's southern delta regions managed to coexist so peacefully for centuries. That sojourn brought aish baladi to Alfheim. Along with this delicious bread, the Elves learned that racial strife is not some relentless, implacable force of destiny. Unfortunately, they have yet to fully embrace the lesson.

DIFFICULTY: Medium

PREP TIME: 30 minutes, plus 2 hours 40 minutes to rest

COOK TIME: 8 minutes

YIELD: 6 servings

DIETARY NOTES: Vegan

INGREDIENTS:

1 cup (237 milliliters) water

2 teaspoons (7 grams) active dry yeast

2¼ cups (330 grams) whole wheat flour, plus more if needed

2 teaspoons (8 grams) salt

1 teaspoon (5 grams) sugar

¼ cup (15 grams) wheat bran

Combine the water and yeast in a large bowl. Mix well and set aside for 10 minutes, or until the yeast has become active, and it looks frothy.

Add the flour, salt, and sugar. Mix until it just comes together. If the dough is too sticky, add 1 tablespoon of wheat flour at a time until it becomes tacky. Knead the dough for 5 minutes and shape into a ball.

Transfer the dough ball into a large, oiled bowl. Cover the bowl with plastic wrap and let the dough rest until it has doubled in size, about 2 hours.

Place wheat bran on a plate and set aside. Line a baking sheet with parchment paper.

Transfer the raised dough to a lightly floured countertop. Lightly pat the dough and divide it into 6 equal pieces.

Tuck in the sides and form each piece into a ball. Roll out to circles 5 inches (13 centimeters) wide. Place each rolled-out dough on the wheat bran and press down. Transfer each piece, wheat bran side down, onto the baking sheet. Cover the dough with a towel and let rest for 30 minutes.

Preheat the oven to 500°F (260°C). Bake until puffed up and cooked through, about 6 to 8 minutes.

KOFTA

Nearly every realm seems to have a mouthwatering meatball recipe, but this lamb-based one from Alfheim is one of a kind. The smoky aroma of sizzling kofta logs wafting off grills in Alfheim's open food courts always makes me stop and sniff happily. (As a hopeless epicure, I honestly don't care how silly I look indulging my sense of smell.) The unique combination of seasonings also gives Elven kofta an unforgettable flavor too, thanks to its cilantro, minced garlic, and that nut-rich spice mix.

Whenever I travel across Alfheim's countryside—lush and woodsy to the south, sandy and desolate to the north—I'm always struck by the contrast between the warmth of its scattered townships and the slightly severe formality of the great Ringed Temple on the Lake of Light. Elves are a surprisingly communal culture, not at all mysterious in the way they're often portrayed in other realms. True, every Elven township is built on strong familial bonds and shared rituals, so visitors can sometimes feel "outside the circle."

But all you have to do is set a big platter of grilled kofta and a couple pitchers of iced karkade (hibiscus tea) on an outdoor table. Make the universal gesture that says, "Please help me eat this!" Pay special attention to the elders who edge warily forward. Ask them about the local history. Soon enough, you'll be surrounded by an Elven platoon of new friends, singing their ancestral songs.

DIFFICULTY: Easy

PREP TIME: 30 minutes

COOK TIME: 15 minutes, plus 1 hour to cool and at least 3 hours to chill

YIELD: 6 servings

DIETARY NOTES: Dairy-Free, Gluten-Free

INGREDIENTS:

1 shallot

2 cloves garlic, minced

2 tablespoons (4 grams) fresh parsley

1 tablespoon (2 grams) fresh cilantro

1 pound (454 grams) ground lamb

1 teaspoon (4 grams) salt

3 tablespoons (30 grams) Dwarven Spice Mixture (page 16)

1 tablespoon (15 mililiters) olive oil

Place the shallot, garlic, parsley, and cilantro in a food processor. Process until the ingredients are finely chopped. Transfer to a large bowl. Add the ground lamb, salt, and spice mixture. Combine until the ingredients just come together, but do not overwork the meat.

Divide the mixture into 6 portions. Form each portion into a log 4 inches (10 centimeters) long. Lightly brush each of the koftas with olive oil.

Using a grill pan, grill the kofta over medium-high heat for about 5 to 10 minutes, flipping occasionally, until all sides are evenly browned.

SPICY MOUTABEL

◉ ne misconception about Elves is that they prefer bland foods. Where that notion originated, I have no idea—perhaps in Svartalfheim, where Dwarves prefer a spicy kick to everything, including their desserts. (Also, some Dwarves have grievances about anything Elf-related.) This spicy eggplant dip, quite popular in Alfheim, should help put those rumors to rest. The serrano peppers alone are enough to sizzle your tongue. Add in ground Kashmiri pepper plus minced garlic and onions, and you've got a hummus-like dip that will send any dubious Dwarf straight to the nearest ice-water pitcher for a chaser. This spicy moutabel is best when scooped directly into the mouth with fresh, hot pita bread.

DIFFICULTY: Easy

PREP TIME: 30 minutes, plus time to cool and at least 3 hours to chill

COOK TIME: 1 hour

YIELD: 6 servings

DIETARY NOTES: Vegan, Gluten-Free

IN COLLABORATION WITH:
Marc Toscano

INGREDIENTS:

2 eggplants

6 cloves garlic, minced

½ medium onion, minced

3 serrano peppers, tops removed

⅓ cup (85 grams) tahini

1 teaspoon (4 grams) salt

1 teaspoon (2 grams) ground Kashmiri pepper

½ cup (108 grams) olive oil, plus more for serving

2 tablespoons (24 grams) lemon juice

TO MAKE IT LESS SPICY, REMOVE THE SEEDS FROM THE SERRANO PEPPERS.

Preheat the oven to 350°F (177°C). Using a fork, poke several holes in each of the eggplants and rub with olive oil. Place on a 9-by-13-inch (23-by-33-centimeter cm) baking sheet and bake for 1 hour, or until softened. Let cool, remove and discard the skin, and roughly chop into big cubes.

Transfer the eggplant into a food processor with garlic, onions, serrano peppers, tahini, salt, and Kashmiri pepper. Pulse until smooth.

Slowly pour in the olive oil and lemon juice while pulsing the food processor to combine. Transfer to an airtight container and refrigerate for at least 3 hours. Serve topped with olive oil.

KARKADE

Something about hibiscus tea is downright curative. I'm not sure if it has a medicinal quality, or it just tastes so ridiculously good that you can't help but feel better after drinking it. This Elven version of deep-red karkade is a no-nonsense blend of water, sugar, honey, and dried hibiscus flowers. I took this simple recipe from Alfheim and shared it on my travels. Before long, it had become the preferred summer drink of Egyptian pharaohs. Iced karkade is the perfect way to cool down a heated diplomatic session. I like to add a sprig of fresh mint as a garnish.

DIFFICULTY: Easy

PREP TIME: 10 minutes, plus 1 hour to cool and 8 hours to chill

COOK TIME: 20 minutes

YIELD: 8 servings

DIETARY NOTES: Vegetarian, Gluten-Free

INGREDIENTS:

10 cups (2.3 liters) water

½ cup (100 grams) sugar

¼ cup (85 grams) honey

1½ cups (100 grams) dried hibiscus flowers

Combine water, sugar, and honey in a medium pot over medium-high heat. Whisk together until the sugar dissolves. Bring to a boil and remove from the heat.

Add the hibiscus and let steep uncovered for 15 minutes. Strain into a pitcher and discard the hibiscus. Let cool completely before refrigerating overnight.

VANAHEIM

Vanaheim is a stunning land—lush, fertile, thick with woods, bursting with iridescent blossoms, and teeming with wildlife. The Vanir people, gods all, are deeply attuned to the natural world. Gardens abound in their settlements. Vanir-grown fruits and vegetables, touched by seiðr magic, were once the most prized produce in the Nine Realms. And Vanir cookery was seen as downright alchemy, amongst the finest in the world.

Sadly, ever since the crazed All-Father sealed off Vanaheim and forbade travel to or from the verdant realm, food lovers can only tap fading memories of Vanir culinary genius.

Some of my very favorite dishes originated in Vanir kitchens, and I include those recipes here. I must say, however, one reason I love Vanir cuisine is because I associate it so closely with the occasion where I first encountered so much of it: the wedding of Freya and Odin. The overwhelming sense of well-being attached to that remarkable event lingers in my soul to this very day, despite the marriage's ultimate failure and the ugliness of subsequent developments.

Back then, as a God of War whose secret passion was the proliferation of peace and harmony between all races, I saw the ceremony as a culmination of my dreams, a true apotheosis. Years of senseless carnage

between Aesir and Vanir cousins—a grim, bloody engagement called the "Long War" that never moved far from stalemate in either direction—came to an end with a simple recitation of wedding vows in a serene Vanaheim glade.

I'd long lobbied Odin and my kin for a cessation of Aesir-Vanir hostilities. Yet full credit for this shrewd proposal goes to Mimir, the All-Father's closest adviser. Like me, Mimir had grown tired of witnessing the harrowing losses on both sides. His well-earned reputation as a clever yet eminently fair negotiator convinced Vanir envoys to work with him.

I was there at the table when Mimir suddenly leaned to them and said, "Say, how about we marry off our lad to your lass?"

It was brilliant. Odin and Freya! Wed the fierce Aesir king to the powerful, deeply respected Vanir goddess. Both sides were instantly giddy at the prospect of a lasting truce buttressed by such a union. It was agreed that the couple would dwell in Asgard, but the ceremony would take place in Freya's homeland.

Odin directed me to Vanaheim to assist in the arrangements. But I must admit, I've never felt more delightfully useless in my life. The Vanir needed no help from me. They attacked wedding preparations with the same exuberant abandon I'd seen on the battlefield, turning the ceremony into a joyous, realm-wide outdoor festival. I watched Vanir sorcerers sling seiðr enchantments right and left, at one point weaving a living tapestry of wildflowers into a natural bower for the vows. I'd never seen such natural beauty, nor such respect for it.

And the postnuptial banquet—good gracious, I've never seen such a feast, not before nor since.

This section lists some of the recipes I stole from the Vanir staff. (I'm joking, of course; the cooks happily shared them with me.) There were sumptuous serving vessels of sea bass and lamb, escorted by hefty platters of shaved sprouts, plus whole roasted carrots and potatoes. An amazingly light pomegranate ambrosia glittered in the champagne goblets. As I snacked on prosciutto-wrapped fig appetizers and watched the phalanx of food march into the fray, I felt a deep sense of relief unlike any I'd ever felt.

All I could think was: Vanir and Aesir, once foes, now eat and drink together like family. The war is over. It seemed like a validation of all my beliefs.

During the wedding's food preparation, I stepped into the Vanir kitchen. I wanted to whip up a bit of Asgardian fare to placate some of my grumbling Aesir brethren who'd be attending, to give them a small taste of home. Before I could ask, I looked around. Half of the staff was preparing Vanir dishes. The other half was preparing Asgardian fare . . . huge mounds of it! And they did so with an expertise that shocked me!

I sampled the smoked salmon dip, lamb riblets, wild boar ragù, and our traditional köttbullar, or meatballs with cream gravy. (See the recipes in my Asgard chapter.) I was absolutely astounded. These dishes were as tasty as the cooking back home! As I lingered over the familiar smells and flavors, I had a moment of epiphany. I had already sensed the importance of dining as part of diplomacy. But it struck me that few things show more respect for a culture than to appreciate and master its native dishes.

I vowed to always honor my dinner guests in this manner, by serving them familiar foods while encouraging them to try more exotic tastes too. After all, not everyone is as adventurous as I am!

PROSCIUTTO-WRAPPED FIGS

Given Freya's profound friendship with Hildisvíni, the boar shapeshifter, I admit it surprised me to find a ham-based appetizer so popular in her home realm. Beloved by Vanir at ceremonial rituals such as weddings and spring festivals, this simple starter has a primordial appeal. I hope Hildisvíni has made his peace with it!

DIFFICULTY: Easy

PREP TIME: 10 minutes

COOK TIME: 10 minutes

YIELD: 24 servings

DIETARY NOTES: Gluten-Free

INGREDIENTS:

2 tablespoons (32 grams) balsamic vinegar

1 tablespoon (21 grams) honey

12 mission figs, halved

3 ounces (85 grams) Brie cheese, cut into 24 portions

8 slices prosciutto, cut into three strips each

Preheat the oven to 425°F (218°C). Line a baking sheet with parchment paper.

Whisk the balsamic vinegar and honey in a small bowl. Brush the insides of each fig with the honey balsamic vinegar, reserving some for serving. Place a portion of Brie on top of each brushed fig.

Take a prosciutto slice and wrap it around a fig. Place on the baking sheet. Repeat with the remaining prosciutto and figs.

Bake for 10 minutes. Serve with the remaining honey balsamic vinegar.

SHAVED BRUSSELS SPROUTS SALAD

I once joined a Vanir hunting party as part of a cultural exchange effort I'd arranged between Asgard and Vanaheim—a largely doomed effort, of course. But despite some competitive tension between my Aesir kin and our Vanir guides, that expedition into a foreign realm's wilderness was quite enjoyable. When we encamped the very first evening, our hosts prepared a multi-course spread that was most remarkable for a campfire meal. It started with this tasty pre-prepared dish. I will admit, until I sampled this salad, I was not a fan of Brussels sprouts. After that, I broke out the recipe whenever I wanted to kickstart an important diplomatic banquet. It never fails me!

DIFFICULTY: Easy

PREP TIME: 30 minutes

YIELD: 6 servings

DIETARY NOTES: Vegetarian, Gluten-Free

INGREDIENTS:

DRESSING:

3 tablespoons (44 grams) lemon juice

2 teaspoons (3 grams) lemon zest

1½ tablespoons (26 grams) apple cider vinegar

2 tablespoons (42 grams) honey

1 tablespoon (15 grams) Dijon mustard

½ teaspoon (2 grams) garlic powder

½ teaspoon (2 grams) ginger powder

⅓ cup (75 grams) olive oil

Salt

Black pepper

SALAD:

1 small Granny Smith apple, peeled, cored, and chopped

1 teaspoon (5 grams) lemon juice

1 pound (454 grams) Brussels sprouts, thinly sliced

3 ounces (86 grams) arugula, thinly sliced

¼ cup (25 grams) walnuts, chopped, plus more for serving

¼ cup (40 grams) dried cherries, chopped, plus more for serving

⅓ cup (30 grams) Parmesan cheese, finely shredded, plus more for serving

To make the dressing: Whisk together lemon juice and zest, vinegar, honey, mustard, garlic powder, and ginger powder in a medium bowl. Slowly pour in the olive oil while whisking vigorously. Season with salt and pepper to taste. Use immediately or store in an airtight container in the refrigerator for up to 1 week. The oil will separate after sitting for a while, so be sure to whisk before serving.

To make the salad: Toss the chopped apple in the lemon juice in a large bowl. Add all the salad ingredients and mix until fully combined. Add the dressing and toss to coat the salad. Serve with more walnuts, dried cherries, and Parmesan cheese to your liking.

CHILEAN SEA BASS

◆

The seas and waterways of Vanaheim are just as gorgeous and wild as the realm's land features. Schools of sea bass can be found in abundance, and with a bit of seiðr enchantment, the fishing is always good. This moderately difficult dish is a staple of Vanir family feasts, and it appears frequently at public festivals as well. Exporting this recipe to other cultures has been one of my secret goals for years!

DIFFICULTY: Medium

PREP TIME: 30 minutes, plus 18 hours to marinate

COOK TIME: 20 minutes

YIELD: 4 servings

DIETARY NOTES: N/A

◇

INGREDIENTS:

SEA BASS MARINADE:

¼ cup (52 grams) mirin

2 teaspoons (10 grams) soy sauce

2 tablespoons (32 grams) white miso

1 tablespoon (21 grams) honey

1 teaspoon (5 grams) sesame oil

2 cloves garlic, minced

1-inch (2½-centimeter) piece of ginger, minced

1 pound (454 grams) Chilean sea bass, cut into 4 equal portions

BOK CHOY:

1 teaspoon (5 grams) canola oil

1 pound baby bok choy, with stems and leaves separated, then chopped

2 teaspoons (10 grams) mirin

MUSHROOMS:

1 teaspoon (5 grams) canola oil

2 king oyster mushrooms, sliced

½ teaspoon (2½ grams) sesame oil

FOR ASSEMBLY:

6½ ounces (184 grams) soba noodles, cooked

Black and white sesame seeds, for garnish

2 scallions, finely chopped, for garnish

To marinate the sea bass: Whisk the mirin, soy sauce, white miso, honey, sesame oil, garlic, and ginger in a small bowl. Transfer to a sealable bag with the sea bass. Let marinate in the refrigerator for at least 18 hours, and up to 24 hours.

Preheat the oven to 425°F (218°C). Line a baking sheet with parchment paper. Remove the fish from the marinade and place on the baking sheet. Bake for 15 minutes, or until cooked through.

To make the bok choy: Heat a small frying pan with canola oil over medium-high heat. Add the bok choy stems and cook until softened, about 3 minutes. Add the bok choy leaves and cook until wilted, about 1 minute. Add the mirin and cook for another 2 minutes until the mirin is absorbed. Set aside.

To make the mushrooms: Heat a small frying pan with canola oil over medium-high heat. Add the king oyster mushrooms and cook until golden brown, about 7 to 9 minutes. Remove from the heat, add the sesame oil, and toss together.

For assembly: To prepare each portion, place a fourth of the soba on a plate, top with one-fourth of the bok choy and the mushrooms. Place a portion of sea bass on top and garnish with sesame seeds and scallions.

RACK OF LAMB

◆

The Vanir version of this classic is my personal favorite. I first tasted this succulent dish during the dinner break of a Vanaheim council meeting in Njörð's seaside longhouse. Marveling at the juicy tenderness (for even a competent cook can produce dry and chewy lamb) I made my way into the kitchen and started asking questions. There, I learned the keys to success are: 1. the oiled spice rub beforehand, 2. using a leaner cut of meat in a hotter oven, and 3. the fat-crisping broil at the end.

DIFFICULTY: Medium

PREP TIME: 1 hour, plus 1 hour to rest

COOK TIME: 40 minutes

YIELD: 4 servings

DIETARY NOTES: Gluten-Free, Dairy-free

◆

INGREDIENTS:

8 cloves garlic, minced

1½ tablespoons (9 grams) Spartan Spice Mixture (page 19)

2 teaspoons (8 grams) salt

1 teaspoon (2 grams) black pepper

3 tablespoons (41 grams) olive oil

1 teaspoon (5 grams) red wine vinegar

One 2-pound (908-gram) rack of lamb

Combine the garlic, Spartan spice, salt, pepper, olive oil, and red wine vinegar in a bowl. Rub the mixture all over the lamb meat. Line a baking sheet with aluminum foil and top with a wire rack. Place the lamb on the wire rack, fat side up. Let rest at room temperature for 45 minutes.

Preheat the oven to 450°F (232°C). Roast the lamb until it reaches the desired temperature on an instant-read thermometer:

MEDIUM-RARE: 125°F (52°C), about 25 minutes
MEDIUM: 135°F (57°C), about 30 minutes
MEDIUM-WELL: 140°F (60°C), about 35 minutes

Turn the broiler on high and cook until the fat begins to crisp up, about 2 to 4 minutes. Remove from the oven and cover in foil. Let rest for 10 minutes. To serve, use a sharp knife and cut portions between the bones.

WHOLE ROASTED CARROTS

◆

The annual Harvest Moon Festival in Vanaheim spans the realm from border to border. You won't see a more spectacular display of fresh produce in any market, anywhere. If you love cooking and preparing meals with perfectly ripe fruits and vegetables, the festival is like a chef's version of Valhalla! The ancient Vanir sorcery conjures a luscious yield in just a matter of days. I'm particularly fond of the carrots. A handful of these brilliant orange Vanir taproots can put a fresh spin on any meal. This basic Vanir recipe brushes a honey/curry mix onto cut carrots then roasts them in a kiln.

DIFFICULTY: Easy

PREP TIME: 20 minutes

COOK TIME: 30 minutes

YIELD: 4 servings

DIETARY NOTES: Vegetarian, Gluten-Free

◇

INGREDIENTS:

¼ cup (53 grams) olive oil

2 tablespoons (42 grams) honey

1 tablespoon (8 grams) Curry Spice Mixture (page 23)

1 teaspoon (4 grams) salt

1½ pounds (681 grams) whole carrots, peeled and cut into 4-inch (10-centimeter) long pieces

Nonstick spray

Preheat the oven to 425°F (218°C). Prepare a baking sheet with aluminum foil and nonstick spray. Whisk the olive oil, honey, curry mixture, and salt in a medium bowl. Place the carrots on the baking sheet and brush both sides with the honey curry mixture.

Bake for 15 minutes, flip the carrots over and bake for another 15 minutes. Keep warm until ready to serve.

IF THE SAUCE SEEMS TOO THICK, RUB THE SAUCE INTO THE CARROTS WITH YOUR HANDS. DON'T BE AFRAID TO GET YOUR HANDS A LITTLE DIRTY WHEN WORKING IN THE KITCHEN.

ROASTED POTATOES

◆

Vanaheim is a wild, beautiful land. I've heard Mimir call it "a realm blessed in bounty," and nothing exhibits that quite like the spread at a Vanir nuptial feast. What could be more fundamental to the natural order than a bountiful crock of potatoes sliced, tossed in oil and spice, and flame roasted to perfection in Vanaheim's signature kiln ovens? Over the years, I find that the multicolored presentation of cubed red, white, purple, and sweet potato also adds to the enchantment of the dish.

DIFFICULTY: Easy

PREP TIME: 20 minutes

COOK TIME: 40 minutes

YIELD: 4 servings

DIETARY NOTES: Vegan, Gluten-Free

◆

INGREDIENTS:

¼ cup (55 grams) olive oil

2 tablespoons (8 grams) Jötunn Spice Mixture (page 15)

2 teaspoons (8 grams) salt

3 medium red potatoes, cut into large cubes

2 medium white potatoes, cut into large cubes

2 medium sweet potatoes, peeled and cut into large cubes

1 medium purple sweet potato, peeled and cut into large cubes

Nonstick spray

Preheat the oven to 425°F (218°C). Prepare a baking sheet with aluminum foil and nonstick spray. Whisk the olive oil, Jötunn Spice Mixture, and salt in a large bowl.

Toss the potatoes in the seasoned oil. Place the oiled potatoes on the baking sheet. Bake for 20 minutes, toss the potatoes around, and bake for another 15 minutes. Keep warm until ready to serve.

BAKLAVA MINI TARTS

◆

B aklava can be a difficult pastry for inexperienced cooks to master, but the result is more than worth the effort. If you get the recipe right, these tarts are a treat without equal. One particularly cold Fimbulwinter day, I remember being in the kitchen at Sindri's house in the Realm Between Realms, chopping sweet nut toppings, browning butter, and carefully slicing up strips of phyllo dough. What an exacting process it was! The geometry of the dough prep alone is complicated, and must be done with mathematical precision. I was pleased that despite his fastidious fear of touching things, Sindri seemed to enjoy every step.

That evening, as our mini tarts baked, Sindri told me it smelled like Freya's kitchen in Midgard's Sanctuary Grove—cinnamon and cardamom. He told me how her kitchen window granted a magical view of Vanaheim. It saddened me that, despite Midgard's own vast tracts of natural beauty, Freya's longing for her homeland was still so compelling.

DIFFICULTY: Hard

PREP TIME: 45 minutes, plus 4 hours to rest

COOK TIME: 45 minutes

YIELD: 9 tarts

DIETARY NOTES: Vegetarian

INGREDIENTS:

½ cup (112 grams) butter

1 cup (135 grams) pistachios

1½ cups (140) walnuts

½ teaspoon (1 gram) ground cinnamon

¼ teaspoon (½ gram) ground cardamom

¼ cup (57 grams) sugar

Twelve 9-by-14-inch (23-by-36 centimeter) phyllo dough sheets, defrosted, plus one more if desired

SYRUP:

⅓ cup (79 mililiters) water

½ cup (116 grams) sugar

½ cup (170 grams) honey

2 tablespoons (30 grams) lemon juice

Melt the butter in a medium saucepan over medium heat. Cook while occasionally swirling the butter until it becomes golden brown, about 10 minutes. Pour the butter into a cup and let it cool.

Place the pistachios, walnuts, cinnamon, cardamom, and sugar in a food processor. Pulse until the nuts are chopped. Set aside.

Preheat the oven to 350°F (177°C). Prepare a muffin pan by brushing some of the butter in 9 of the muffin holes.

Take a sheet of phyllo dough and brush it with the butter. Take another phyllo sheet and press it down against the buttered sheet. Brush over the top with more butter. Repeat until there are 4 layers of phyllo dough and butter.

Lay the prepared phyllo dough lengthwise and divide into 4-inch (10-centimeter) wide strips. You should have three 4-inch (10-centimeter) strips and one 2-inch (5-centimeter) strip. Take each large strip and cut it in half so that you have two rectangles that are 4-by-4½ inches (10-by-11 centimeters). Cut the 2-inch (5-centimeter) strip into 4 roughly square portions.

Continued on page 72

Continued from page 71

To create the base of one pastry, take one of the six rectangles and brush with the butter. Place another rectangle, turned 45° so the corners do not align, on top and press down. Repeat this with the remaining rectangles until you have 3 X-shaped bases for 3 tarts.

Stuff one of the bases inside one of the muffin pan's cups and press it down. Fill the cup halfway up with the nut mixture. Take one of the small phyllo squares and press it on top of the nuts. Add nut mixture until level with the top of the muffin tin. If desired, you can top these with more phyllo dough by cutting a sheet into nine rectangles, one for each tart.

Repeat steps 4 to 7 until there are 9 baklava tarts.

Bake the tarts for 25 minutes, until the phyllo dough has turned golden brown.

To make the syrup: While the phyllo dough is baking, combine water, sugar, honey, and lemon juice in a medium saucepan over medium-high heat. Whisk until the sugar has dissolved and bring to a boil. Reduce the heat and simmer for 10 minutes. Remove from the heat and set aside.

Once the tarts have finished baking, immediately spoon half of the syrup into the tarts and let rest for 1 minute. Pour the remaining syrup over the tarts while making sure not to drown them. Let set for 4 hours at room temperature. Transfer to an airtight container and store at room temperature for up to 2 weeks.

AMBROSIA

◆

Traditionally, ambrosia is known as the "libation of the gods" and is associated with immortality. This pomegranate-based Vanir recipe is so good that I'd have to say it qualifies. Put two tablespoons of the syrup with muddled mint in a flute of champagne, knock it back, and live forever.

DIFFICULTY: Easy

PREP TIME: 5 minutes, plus 12 hours to chill

COOK TIME: 30 minutes

YIELD: 12 servings

DIETARY NOTES: Vegan, Gluten-Free

INGREDIENTS:

POMEGRANATE SYRUP:

½ cup (118 grams) pomegranate juice

¼ cup (57 grams) sugar

2 tablespoons (30 grams) lime juice

FOR EACH DRINK:

2 fresh mint leaves

1 tablespoon (10 grams) pomegranate seeds

2 tablespoons (30 grams) pomegranate syrup

Champagne

To make the syrup: Combine the pomegranate juice, sugar, and lime juice in a small saucepan and place over medium-high heat. Whisk until the sugar has dissolved and it reaches a boil.

Reduce the heat and simmer for 10 minutes. Remove from the heat and allow to cool. Strain into an airtight container, cover, and refrigerate for at least 12 hours, and up to 2 weeks.

To make each drink: Lightly muddle the mint in a champagne flute. Add the pomegranate seeds and syrup. Top with enough champagne to fill the glass.

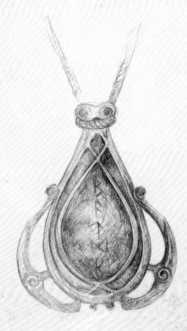

ASGARD

Asgard is the feasting capital of the realms, hands down. We Aesir gods—and yes, despite all the atrocities and rash, cruel leadership, I still consider them my tribe—feast with the same reckless abandon that we fight. Our dining halls are legendary. So, if you plan to write a cookbook, Asgard is certainly a good place to find a trove of recipes.

I'm not just being partial to my homeland when I say Asgard is truly a stunning realm. Many visitors over the years have rendered that same judgment, calling it the Golden Land. True to the lore, Asgard sat in the very highest branches of Yggdrasil. Glorious dwelling-places of the gods dotted Asgard's rolling hills, each one a citadel with living quarters, armory, and a cavernous feasting hall within. Odin's own dwelling was the jewel of the realm, and he was known to have surveyed all lands from there.

Truth be told, I haven't seen my home in more years than I can count. Yet as I write this, my mind's eye sees it clearly, peering through memory as if it were a mountain stream.

Do you know the story of how the Aesir-Vanir war actually started? I think it reveals basic aspects of Asgardian culture.

The Aesir and Vanir have never liked each other. Some say the enmity traces back to the very moment the two tribes emerged from Ymir's mystic lifeblood—in other words, back to when time itself began. After eons of smoldering tension, the Vanir god

Freyr—son of Vanir king Njörð, brother of Freya, and beloved of his people—decided enough was enough. He sent a courier to Odin, offering to discuss terms of a more peaceful coexistence. Odin accepted, and he invited Freyr to Asgard.

Freyr arrived with a truly generous good-faith gift: he taught us how to increase crop yields using Vanir magic. But before Freyr and Odin could discuss peace terms, Aesir farmers (soused on mead, most likely) lost control of the seiðr enchantments and poisoned their own crops. Naturally, the drunken fools blamed Freyr, calling his "gift" an attempt to sabotage their harvest. With typical Aesir impulsivity, a drunken Thor rallied a mob that tossed the Vanir god into a huge pile of poisoned crops, set it on fire, and staggered back to Asgard's taverns to drink themselves deeper into stupefaction. Meanwhile, Freyr conjured a protective spell and escaped the inferno. Then he sneaked out of Asgard and returned home.

Back in Vanaheim, Freyr's situation report triggered rage and calls for vengeance. The Vanir leadership quickly declared a state of all-out war against the Aesir.

Thus began the Long War of the Gods. Such meaningless slaughter!

Most Aesir are physically powerful gods who fling themselves with berserk fury at foes, relying on brute force and brutal weaponry. But Vanir magicks are truly powerful and quite frightening. Relentless Odin would

deploy a hundred troopships only to have Njörð summon fierce hurricane winds to sink the fleet. The Vanir sorcerer Lýtir would cast confusion spells on any Aesir who washed up alive on Vanaheim's shores, driving them to hack and hew at each other. If any Aesir warrior survived long enough to reach a Vanaheim settlement, the reckoning was swift and bloody.

This sort of thing went on for many, many years. Both sides suffered horrific casualties. Neither side could gain the upper hand. As losses mounted, I consulted with Mimir, the only member of Odin's inner circle I could really trust. We made secret overtures to Vanir envoys, but Odin rejected every proposed solution. He saw truce as defeat, which is the very essence of

Aesir thinking, I'm afraid.

Fortunately, Odin was also deeply smitten by the sight of Freya on the battlefield, so terrifying and beautiful. When the All-Father made a stray comment to that effect one day (his mind lubricated to a rosy flush by Asgardian glogg, no doubt), Mimir's Bifröst eyes glowed with sudden shrewd insight.

That's when he first came up with his idea of a union: Odin and Freya, the ultimate power couple.

Here's another quick story that reveals much about Asgard. Amongst the Aesir, this tale is known as "Hrimthur's Favor." It involves the two things Odin fears most: Ragnarök and the Giants.

I've mentioned Thamur, the Giant stonemason. Considered the greatest mason in all the realms, Thamur erected the impenetrable Great Walls of Jötunheim. Before Thor caught up with the stone-wright near the port of Njörðholm in Midgard and murdered him, using his hammer to drive the Giant's own chisel right through his skull, Thamur was father to a son named Hrimthur.

The mason's boy was so distraught by his father's weighty shadow, and made one grand, unique attempt to make a name for himself elsewhere. One day, slipping away from Thamur's watchful eye, a young Hrimthur donned a disguise to visit Asgard and requested an audience with the All-Father himself. There, Hrimthur offered to build a new, impregnable wall around Asgard in just two years, claiming that their existing wall was flimsy—it wasn't Jötunn work, afterall. If he failed to meet this seemingly impossible deadline, his work would be free of charge. If Hrimthur succeeded, he asked to be awarded with recognition and accolades that might match even his father's. I was there in Odin's throne room when Hrimthur proposed these terms. I admit, I was amused—the task of walling Asgard's capital city would take decades for any normal stone-wright. Odin thought so too, so he quickly accepted the deal. But as the mason got started, a great flying stallion suddenly joined him. This horse could deliver masonry materials as fast as Hrimthur could work … which, by the way, was amazingly fast. Over the next few months, I'd sit at my window, watching the walls go up with lightning speed. I was so impressed, I found myself secretly rooting for Hrimthur. I'd have the palace kitchen staff prepare some of our best dishes for his meal breaks—he became a big fan of our wild boar ragú washed down with a goblet of Asgardian honeyed spirits.

Hrimthur finished the job with plenty of time to spare and unexpectedly asked to change his request for completing the wall. Instead of accolades that might out-shine even Thamur, Hrimthur requested a meeting with Odin's queen, Freya.

Odin, never one to give praise when he didn't have to, agreed and quickly sent Freya to meet him, but all Hrimthur did was whisper something in her ear. Then he exited Asgard, vowing to never return again.

The question remains: What did Hrimthur whisper to Freya? Only she knows, and she's never revealed it. Mimir suspects it has something to do with a weakness in Asgard's wall—"structural or perhaps magical," he says—purposely engineered by Hrimthur.

Leaving such knowledge with Lady Freya is quite an irony. Today, few hate Odin and the Aesir worse than she does.

SMOKED SALMON DIP

I'll try not to be biased, but I honestly consider Asgard as the food capital of the world. And it starts right here, with this perfect appetizer dip that has no equal, not anywhere. Maybe it's the subtle ratio of horseradish to fish sauce, or the combination of sour cream and cream cheese in perfect balance with the citrus and scallions. Whatever the case, I never tire of this starter dish and sometimes eat too much. I once watched an Aesir cousin gorge on so much dip at a solstice banquet that we had to carry him back to his guestroom. It was well before the main course of lamb riblet platters arrived, which was a terrible shame.

DIFFICULTY: Easy

PREP TIME: 30 minutes, plus 2 hours to chill

YIELD: 6 servings

DIETARY NOTES: N/A

INGREDIENTS:

8 ounces (226 grams) cream cheese

2 ounces (57 grams) sour cream

2 scallions, chopped

1½ tablespoons (35 grams) horseradish

1 tablespoon (15 grams) lemon juice

1 teaspoon (2 grams) lemon zest

¼ teaspoon (1¼ grams) fish sauce

¼ teaspoon (1 gram) salt

¼ teaspoon (½ gram) black pepper

5 ounces (140 grams) smoked salmon

Whisk together the cream cheese and sour cream in a medium bowl.

Add the other ingredients and mix until just combined. Place in an airtight container and refrigerate for 2 hours before serving. Store in the refrigerator for up to 1 week.

LAMB RIBLETS

◆

Go light on appetizer dip if you've got these riblets up next on the dinner menu! Given the complexity of flavors when eating this dish, it has a surprisingly easy preparation. The secret, in my book—and this *is* my book—is the blending of the curry spice mix with the brushed coatings of tonkatsu sauce. The subtleties of the flavors released into one's palate is a revelation. Okay, maybe I'm overstating it a bit, but this kiln-baked lamb platter, layered atop a bed of sliced onion and garlic, is probably Asgard's signature dish. I can't imagine a special event without it.

For example, I remember a great feast called by Odin to celebrate what seemed a decisive Aesir victory in the Long War. Magni and Modi, the dim but deadly sons of Thor, had felled the powerful goddess Nerthus, a particularly skilled Vanir sorceress. (They prevailed through sheer dumb luck, as far as I could tell.) Thus Odin, Thor, and many of the greatest Aesir warriors—Hoenir, Ve, Vili, and Hodr—gathered in Odin's silver hall of Valaskjálf. We washed down those remarkable Asgardian lamb riblets with the finest meads in the realm. It was a joyful night for warrior gods.

The next day, hungover and overconfident, Odin deployed a mighty Aesir horde onto the plains of Vanaheim, seeking to crush the Vanir once and for all. But in a flash (literally) the Aesir were swept away—the whole lot, every soldier—by a terrifying seiðr torrent conjured up by a vengeful Njörð and his Vanir council, including Freya. Just like that, the Long War had returned to deadlock.

DIFFICULTY: Easy
PREP TIME: 20 minutes
COOK TIME: 3 to 4 hours
YIELD: 6 servings
DIETARY NOTES: Gluten-Free

◆

INGREDIENTS:

½ medium onion, sliced

3 cloves garlic, sliced

¼ cup (59 mililiters) water

2 pounds (907 grams) lamb riblets

2 tablespoons (26 grams) olive oil

1½ tablespoons (10 grams) Curry Spice Mix (page 23)

1 tablespoon (10 grams) salt

½ teaspoon (1 gram) black pepper

2 teaspoons (10 grams) light brown sugar

½ cup (144 grams) tonkatsu sauce

Preheat the oven to 250°F (121°C). Line a deep baking pan with aluminum foil. Layer the onion and garlic at the bottom of the pan. Add the water.

Place the lamb riblets in a medium bowl with the olive oil. Toss until all the riblets are covered in oil. Combine the curry mixture, salt, pepper, and brown sugar in a small bowl. Sprinkle the spice mixture over the riblets and rub until covered.

Place the lamb on top of the onions and garlic in the pan. Cover with aluminum foil and bake until tender, about 2 to 3 hours.

Remove the top layer of foil and brush the ribs with a third of the tonkatsu. Return to the oven and cook, uncovered, for 10 minutes.

Remove from the oven again and brush the lamb with another third of the tonkatsu. Turn on the broiler and place the pan just below the broiler. Cook for 5 minutes, until the meat begins to crisp. Take it out, flip the meat, brush with the remaining tonkatsu, and place back under the broiler for another 5 minutes and serve hot.

KÖTTBULLAR

◆

Every realm seems to have a distinctive and delectable entry in the meatball category. This is Asgard's version. Köttbullar just *sounds* meaty and appetizing, doesn't it? I don't wish to be crude, but I can barely say the name without salivating. One admission, however: When I say this is an Asgardian recipe, the truth is that köttbullar came here by way of a faerie kingdom on an island somewhere in the wilds of Midgard. Yes, it arrived in the pocket of a young troublemaker by the name of Mimir.

I distinctly remember the first time I met Mimir, many years ago. I was a young god, still trying to define my role as the Aesir God of War. One day, Odin called together his full court and council, and then introduced this strange horn-headed fellow as "the smartest man I've ever met!" Mimir's suspect past as a faerie king's court jester, errand boy, and admitted "knavish sprite" didn't give me a lot of confidence in his advisory capacity. But his intelligence was immediately apparent, and soon enough, I discovered that we shared an unsettling number of common sensibilities.

Over time, Mimir became a great ally in my ongoing struggle to demilitarize Odin's worldview. Though Odin considered Mimir his primary ambassador to other realms, in fact the so-called Smartest Man Alive was my close partner in the prodigious task of (as he called it) "protecting Odin from himself." We spent many a late night trying to chart a course around the All-Father's dangerous Ragnarök obsessions and increasingly genocidal impulses over bowls of köttbullar and goblets of glogg.

DIFFICULTY: Medium
PREP TIME: 45 minutes
COOK TIME: 30 minutes
YIELD: 8 servings
DIETARY NOTES: N/A

◇

INGREDIENTS:

MEATBALLS:

2 tablespoons (28 grams) unsalted butter

2 medium shallots, chopped

3 cloves garlic, minced

1 pound (454 grams) ground lamb

1 pound (454 grams) ground pork

¾ cup (52 grams) panko bread crumbs

1 egg

1 teaspoon (4 grams) salt

½ teaspoon (1 gram) black pepper

2 teaspoons (3 grams) Jötunn Spice Mixture (page 15)

2 tablespoons (10 grams) fresh parsley

1 tablespoon (15 mililiters) canola oil

GRAVY:

3 tablespoons (54 grams) unsalted butter

¼ cup (44 grams) all-purpose flour

2 cups (473 grams) beef broth

1 cup (227 grams) sour cream

2 teaspoons (11 grams) Dijon mustard

Black pepper

Salt

Lingonberry jam, for serving

Continued on page 86

Continued from page 85

To make the meatballs: Melt the butter in a large frying pan over medium-high heat. Add the shallots and cook until just softened, about 5 minutes. Add the garlic and cook for another 2 minutes. Remove from the heat and place on a plate with a paper towel to drain. Let cool completely.

Combine the ground lamb and pork, panko, egg, salt, pepper, Jötunn spices, parsley, and cooled shallots in a large bowl. Stir until just combined. Form into 1½-inch (4-centimeter) meatballs, about 24 to 32 of them.

Heat a large pan with the canola oil over medium-high heat. Add the meatballs, brown each side, and cook through, about 10 to 15 minutes. Transfer to a plate.

To make the gravy: In the same pan, melt the butter over medium-high heat. Slowly add the flour while constantly whisking.

After it has combined into a roux, about 3 to 4 minutes, slowly add the broth while whisking. Bring to a boil and then reduce the heat. Simmer until the gravy has thickened, about 5 minutes.

Whisk in the sour cream and mustard. Season with pepper and salt to taste. Add the meatballs, mix, and simmer for 8 minutes until the meatballs are heated. Serve with lingonberry jam.

WILD BOAR RAGÙ

◆

Boar hunting is a major pastime in Asgard. One reason is that the hunt itself is such an immensely popular event, featuring two of the things the Aesir love best: drinking and killing things. The second reason is that a wild boar shoulder, properly marinated and prepared, is a culinary treat that's by far the favorite food of Aesir warriors. To be sated with boar then run shrieking into battle is the highest level of existence for some of them.

Our wild boar ragù, made from the shoulder cut, is a remarkably tasty dish found in taverns all across Asgard. The cooking process starts with a 24-hour marination that negates some of that gamey flavor you can get from feral swine. Then a long, slow simmer softens the meat enough to shred into a ragù with the red wine, tomatoes, and other vegetables. Once you've eaten your fill, I recommend a good nap rather than rushing out to slaughter foes.

DIFFICULTY: Medium

PREP TIME: 1 hour, plus 24 hours to marinate

COOK TIME: 5½ hours

YIELD: 6 servings

DIETARY NOTES: Dairy-Free

THIS MARINADE HELPS PULL OUT THE WILD BOAR'S GAMEY FLAVOR.

◇

INGREDIENTS:

MARINADE:

2 pounds (907 grams) wild boar shoulder, cut into large chunks

One 750-milliliter bottle of red wine

5 cloves garlic, smashed

3 bay leaves

20 juniper berries

1 tablespoon (7 grams) black peppercorns

2 sprigs rosemary

2 sprigs thyme

SAUCE:

2 tablespoons (9 grams) olive oil

1 medium onion, diced

2 carrots, peeled and diced

3 celery stalks, diced

6 cloves garlic, diced

2 sardines, deboned

2 cups (473 grams) reserved wine from marinade

28 ounces (794 grams) canned crushed tomatoes

2 cups (473 mililiters) water

1 bay leaf

Pappardelle pasta, for serving

To make the marinade: Combine everything in an airtight container. Refrigerate for at least 24 hours.

The next day, strain everything through a fine mesh strainer. Reserve 2 cups of the wine. Remove the wild boar and discard the spices.

To make the sauce: Heat a Dutch oven with the olive oil over medium-high heat. Add the onions, carrots, and celery. Cook until softened, about 5 to 8 minutes. Add the garlic and sardines and cook for another 2 minutes. Add the wild boar and cook until all sides are browned, about 10 minutes.

Add the reserved wine and cook until the wine has reduced by three-fourths, about 10 minutes. Add the tomatoes, water, and bay leaf. Reduce the heat to low and simmer for 4 to 5 hours until the meat is tender. Using two forks, shred the meat and mix well. Serve with pappardelle pasta.

IF YOU CAN'T FIND A GOOD WILD BOAR, THE SHOULDER OF A DOMESTICATED PIG WILL DO.

SOCKERKRINGLOR

◆

Every Aesir child dreams of sockerkringlor for breakfast every day. Most adults probably do, too. Think of soft baked dough, twisted into a pretzel shape, still warm, slathered in butter, sugar, and vanilla. Your mouth is already watering, is it not? The smell of this pastry got me out of bed on many a winter's morning in Asgard. The same is true now. Sindri is so excited about sockerkringlor that he has the dough ball ready and rising before I can even stumble into the kitchen.

DIFFICULTY: Hard

PREP TIME: 1 hour, plus 1½ hours to rest

COOK TIME: 15 minutes

YIELD: 16 pretzels

DIETARY NOTES: Vegetarian

◆

INGREDIENTS:

3¾ cups (560 grams) all-purpose flour, plus more if needed

½ teaspoon (2 grams) ground cardamom

½ teaspoon (2 grams) salt

1 cup (232 grams) oat milk

Seeds scraped from 1 vanilla bean

2 teaspoons (8 grams) active dry yeast

3 tablespoons (50 grams) sugar

1 egg

6 tablespoons (84 grams) unsalted butter, at room temperature

TOPPING:

1 cup (210 grams) sugar

1 teaspoon (4 grams) ground cardamom

6 tablespoons (84 grams) unsalted butter, melted

Combine the flour, cardamom, and salt in a medium bowl. Set aside.

Combine the oat milk, vanilla bean seeds, yeast, and sugar in a large bowl. Let rest until the yeast becomes active, about 5 minutes. Add the flour mixture and mix together.

As the dough comes together while you begin kneading, add the butter 1 tablespoon at a time. Knead the dough for 5 minutes. If the dough is too sticky, add 1 tablespoon of flour at a time. If it is too dry, add 1 tablespoon of oat milk at a time.

Shape the dough into a ball. Transfer to a large, oiled bowl. Cover and let rise until it has doubled in size, about 1 hour.

Transfer the dough to a lightly floured countertop. Punch down and lightly knead it. Roll out the dough to a 13-by-16-inch (33-by-40-centimeter) rectangle. Cut into 16 equal 1-inch (2½-centimeter) strips.

To form a sockerkringlor, take one of the strips and twist by rolling the ends opposite each other. Once tightly twisted, make an upside-down U shape. Cross the two ends over each other. Take the ends and flip them up over the arch of the U and press down. Place on a parchment-lined backing tray. Repeat with the remaining portions, placing them about 1 inch (2½ centimeters) apart. Cover the sockerkringlor and let rest for 30 minutes.

Preheat the oven to 425°F (218°C). Crack the egg and create an egg wash. Brush it on top of the sockerkringlor. Bake the sockerkringlor until golden, about 13 to 15 minutes.

To make the topping: Combine the sugar and cardamom in a small bowl. Once the sockerkringlor are cooked, use a pastry brush to brush each with the butter, then generously sprinkle with the sugar mixture. Store in an airtight container at room temperature for 2 days.

GLOGG

◆

This hot mulled wine was one of the best weapons in my arsenal of diplomatic firepower. The name itself—*glogg!*—seems so innocuous, conjuring the sound of a slurred word or a drunken attempt to swallow. But one sip of this addictive spiced wine always leads to another, and soon enough all the great emissaries and ambassadors meeting in Týr's Temple would melt into a warm molasses of agreeable camaraderie.

DIFFICULTY: Easy

PREP TIME: 10 minutes

COOK TIME: 20 minutes

YIELD: 4 servings

DIETARY NOTES: Vegan, Gluten-Free

◆

INGREDIENTS:

6 cardamom pods

1 cinnamon stick

1 star anise pod

⅓ cup (74 grams) light brown sugar, packed

1½ cups (343 grams) pomegranate juice

One 750-milliliter bottle of dry red wine

2 large lemons, sliced

1 large orange, sliced

3 figs, halved

3 slices ½-inch thick ginger

Place the cardamom pods cinnamon stick, and star anise in a cheesecloth. Wrap it up and tie it closed with butcher's twine.

Mix the brown sugar, pomegranate juice, and red wine in a large pot over medium-high heat. Whisk together until the sugar has dissolved. Add the spices from the cheesecloth and the remaining ingredients. Bring to a low simmer for 15 minutes. Serve hot.

HONEYED SPIRITS

Mead, and beer, and even glogg are fine for most occasions. But when you want a lighter libation for rounds of toasts at weddings or signing ceremonies, Asgardian honeyed spirits fits the bill. As the name implies, it's a sweet drink, a perfect postprandial cocktail that's elegant, yet friendly. You always want your proceedings, whatever their nature, to leave a pleasant taste in everybody's mouth, do you not?

DIFFICULTY: Easy

PREP TIME: 20 minutes, plus 12 hours 45 minutes to rest

COOK TIME: 15 minutes

YIELD: 12 servings

DIETARY NOTES: Vegetarian, Gluten-Free

INGREDIENTS:

HONEY SYRUP:

¼ cup (60 grams) sugar

½ cup (170 grams) honey

½ cup (119 mililiters) water

4 sprigs thyme

2 sprigs rosemary

FOR EACH DRINK:

Ice, for shaking and for serving

2 ounces (57 grams) gin

½ ounce (14 grams) elderflower liqueur

1 ounce (28 grams) honey syrup

1½ ounces (43 grams) lemon juice

1 lemon slice

To make the syrup: Combine sugar, honey, and water in a medium saucepan and place over medium-high heat. Whisk until the sugar has dissolved and it reaches a boil. Reduce the heat and simmer for 10 minutes.

Remove from the heat and add the thyme and rosemary. Let rest for 45 minutes. Strain into an airtight container. Cover and refrigerate for at least 12 hours, and up to 2 weeks.

For each drink: Fill a cocktail shaker with ice. Add the remaining ingredients and shake vigorously for 10 seconds.

In an old-fashioned glass, add fresh ice and a lemon slice. Pour the mixed drink through a mesh strainer into the glass.

SVARTALFHEIM

Homeland of the Dwarf race, Svartalfheim was sealed off by Odin's nasty barrier spells for many years, just like Vanaheim. The paranoid All-Father's purpose was to prevent Dwarves and Vanir gods from forming any kind of alliance against the Aesir . . . and in this, I suppose, he succeeded. But he also succeeded in making an entire race into another Aesir-hating enemy. Despite his obsession with manipulating the endgame of Ragnarök, Odin was quite poor at long-term strategic thinking—which, of course, is my specialty. Or used to be, anyway. If he'd ever heeded my counsel, maybe the gods wouldn't have faced such a catastrophe.

Another result of sealing Svartalfheim's borders was the spread of odd misperceptions about the realm. Dwarves are typically miners and metalworkers, so people who've never been there (which is most people) assume Svartalfheim is some sort of vast subterranean labor camp lit by the forge fires of surly blacksmiths, or an ugly jumble of deforested badlands beneath smoke-filled skies.

This couldn't be further from the truth. Svartalfheim is, in fact, a truly beautiful land, with skies as blue and woodlands as lush as in any realm. Yes, much activity takes place underground. But most Dwarven settlements sit aboveground, in richly forested canyons. Towns are built around bright cobblestone plazas bustling with food markets and merchants selling textiles, equipment, and other craft items.

Of course, I haven't visited Svartalfheim myself in many years. Things could be different now. But somehow, I doubt it.

Surprisingly little is known about the structure of Dwarven society as well as its customs and traditions. Dwarves do tend to be a secretive lot. And again, while it's true that much work in Svartalfheim takes place in caverns and tunnels, many communal activities tend to be discreet and private as well.

But there is one true thing about Dwarves that *everybody* knows. Dwarves love to eat.

Dwarven food, even when prepared by a good cook (*i.e.*, like Sindri), is generally heavy fare. Dwarves dearly love a distinct sense of "having eaten." Few things make a Dwarf happy quite like a slightly overfull stomach stuffed with sausage rolls or a nice spice-rubbed leg of lamb with crisped-up fat.

That doesn't mean Svartalfheim dishes are brutish or simplistic. You'll find that some of these recipes require a light touch and a refined sense of timing. The Challah Onion Bread, for example, is perhaps my favorite bread in all the realms—but it is not a recipe one tosses together at the last minute on a busy night. A good focus is required, plus a solid hour of prep time.

I remember how, many years ago, the burly Svartalfheim contingent arrived on the Lake of Nine shore, tools in hand, ready to raise a temple. Trust me, you've never seen anyone really work until you see a Dwarf crew at hard labor. For such delicate artisans, they're also relentless and powerful with pick and hammer. Watching them in awe, all I could think was, "These fellows will need a lot of fuel."

Around the lake, I'd set up kitchens and service areas under huge canvas tents for the workers of all races. My support team had amassed several hill-sized mounds of meats, grains, and raw produce in huge lake-cooled storage bins. After watching the hungry Svartalfheim miners and smiths consume their first meal—the word "dine" doesn't really do justice to the carnage I witnessed—I conscripted every hunter I could find, and

sent them up into the Foothills for more game. Much more game.

During that time, I also discovered that Dwarves are surprisingly fond of creative fish recipes. Be sure to check out the awe-inspiring tuna tartare and salmon banh mi dishes I learned from the Svartalfheim cooking staff.

Before moving on to the recipes, I think the Huldra brothers deserve a quick mention.

Like the great inventor Ivaldi and his sons, Brok and Sindri learned their craft in the smithies of Svartalfheim then emigrated to set up shop in other realms. I've known them for many years. Without a doubt, the Huldras can be persnickety and quarrelsome. But even when I complained about their cooking or their stupid arguments, I never forgot that I was speaking with two of the greatest blacksmiths in the realms.

Amazingly, they forged both Mjölnir *and* the Leviathan Axe, the two most powerful and perfectly balanced weapons ever crafted. *Ever.* Think about that. Unfortunately, they gave the hammer to the wrong guy. As Mimir says, "Mjölnir became the bane of Giant-kind." At least they made sure Leviathan ended up in the hands of Laufey the Just.

Look, I used to hate the way Thor picked his teeth after meals, but I would never knock his fighting skill. The same goes for the Huldra brothers. Never underestimate their abilities . . . even though they couldn't bake a decent babka bun to save their lives.

TUNA TARTARE

◆

I learned this fantastic recipe from Dafraeg, a craggy old Dwarf who supervised the kitchen staff for Svartalfheim's Dwarven Council events. Whenever I was in the realm for a Council meeting, I always made sure to step into his kitchen for a visit. He was a sullen, suspicious fellow; the first time I met him, he squinted and told me that diplomacy is "the art of saying *Nice doggy!* until you can find a rock." I took it as a challenge. If I could sway Dafraeg to *any* of my views, I could sway anyone. Plus, I loved to watch him work. He was the finest cook I've ever seen. His expert knifework on the sushi-grade tuna required for this tartare dish was really something to witness.

DIFFICULTY: Medium
PREP TIME: 30 minutes
YIELD: 3 servings
DIETARY NOTES: Dairy-Free

◇

INGREDIENTS:

AVOCADO LAYER:

1½ large, barely ripe avocados, cubed

1 serrano pepper, deseeded and finely minced

½ medium shallot, finely minced

1½ tablespoons (4 grams) fresh cilantro leaves, finely minced

Juice of 1 lime

1 teaspoon (3 grams) black sesame seeds

Salt

Black pepper

TUNA LAYER:

2 cloves garlic, finely minced

1 teaspoon (2 grams) grated ginger

1 teaspoon (5 grams) wasabi paste

2 scallions, green parts only, chopped

1 tablespoon (16 grams) soy sauce

1½ teaspoons (6 grams) sesame oil

1 tablespoon (21 grams) honey

Salt

Black pepper

½ pound sushi-grade tuna, cut into ¼-inch (6-millimeter) cubes

To make the avocado layer: Combine the avocados, peppers, shallots, cilantro, lime juice, and sesame seeds in a medium bowl until it just comes together. Season with salt and pepper. Set aside.

To make the tuna layer: Combine the garlic, ginger, wasabi, scallions, soy sauce, sesame oil, and honey until the wasabi and honey are well incorporated. Season with salt and pepper. Toss with the tuna just before serving.

To assemble each serving, place a 3-inch (7½-centimeter) round cookie cutter on a plate. Place a third of the avocado layer in the cookie cutter and press down with the back of a spoon to make a smooth layer. Top with a third of the tuna and carefully remove the cookie cutter.

SCOTCH EGGS

Whoever invented this intricate appetizer deserves an award, perhaps a statue, or maybe a Jötunn triptych in their honor. Some say Scotch eggs traces to the Dwarven excavation crews who worked the Völunder Mines, back in the days before Andvari unwittingly unleashed his Soul Eater slave-golem on the mining complex. Miners would get stretches of downtime when the digging tapped aquifers and groundwater that needed to be pumped out of the mines. Much of that time was devoted to cooking contests, as Dwarves *really* love eating and good food.

Typically served as an appetizer or picnic food, the traditional Scotch egg is basically a boiled egg coated in a minced or "scotched" potato-whitefish mix and then deep-fried with a breaded outer crust. It's one of the trickiest starter dishes I've ever prepared, and it's also the one that unfailingly draws rave reviews from my guests.

DIFFICULTY: Hard

PREP TIME: 1 hour

COOK TIME: 20 minutes

YIELD: 8 eggs

DIETARY NOTES: N/A

INGREDIENTS:

1 large russet potato, peeled and chopped

Pinch of salt

2 ounces (60 grams) cream cheese, at room temperature

1 teaspoon (5 grams) Dijon mustard

½ ounce (15 grams) scallions, green parts only, finely chopped

Zest of 1 lemon

9 ounces (250 grams) smoked whitefish

8 eggs

¼ cup (28 grams) to ½ cup (56 grams) potato starch

FOR FRYING:

½ cup (115 grams) all-purpose flour

2 eggs, beaten

1½ cups (90 grams) panko breadcrumbs

Peanut oil, for frying

Heat a large pot with potatoes, salt, and just enough water to cover the potatoes over high heat. Bring to a boil, then reduce the heat and simmer for 15 to 20 minutes, or until the potatoes are tender. Drain and place the potatoes in a bowl.

Add the cream cheese, mustard, scallions, and lemon zest. Mash until the potatoes are smooth and well combined with the other ingredients. Fold in the smoked whitefish and mix until just combined. Set aside.

Bring water in a deep pot to a boil over medium-high heat. Carefully place the eight eggs in the water, cover with a lid, and cook for 6½ minutes. For slightly harder egg yolks, increase the time to a maximum of 9 minutes for a completely hard yolk. Immediately remove the pot from the heat and place it under cold running water. Drain and transfer the eggs to a medium bowl with ice cubes and water for about 3 minutes. Carefully remove the eggshells.

Divide the potato mixture into eight equal portions. Take a boiled egg and coat it by rolling it in the potato starch. Take a portion of the potato mixture and flatten it by hand. Place the egg in the center and carefully wrap it around the egg. Repeat this with the remaining eggs.

Continued on page 103

Continued from page 100

Place about 3 inches (7 centimeters) of peanut oil in a deep pot. Preheat oil to 350°F (177°F) over medium-high heat. Make sure when it hits this temperature, you are ready to start frying.

For frying: Set up three stations: a plate with the flour, a bowl with the eggs beaten, and a plate with the panko. Coat each potato-wrapped egg in flour, dip it in the beaten eggs, roll it in the panko, and place it on a plate. If the oil is still heating when you finish the Scotch eggs, refrigerate them until ready.

Once the oil is heated, using a fine-meshed spoon, carefully place two of the balls into the oil. Let cook for 5 minutes until golden brown. Remove and place on a plate with a paper towel to drain, about 5 minutes.

IF YOU ARE WORRIED ABOUT TIMING, START THE PREHEATING AFTER YOU'VE PREPARED THE SCOTCH EGGS FOR FRYING.

CHALLAH ONION BREAD

For some reason, I like caramelized onions in almost anything. For me, it's very nearly an addiction. When I first sampled this braided bread at a Dwarf-hosted banquet, celebrating the activation of the Svartalfheim travel tower on the Lake of Nine's northwest shore, I began accosting people until I found a cook's assistant willing to divulge the recipe. From start to finish, it requires nearly five hours and a number of steps to produce. But if, like me, you relish the process of piecing together an intricate food puzzle, baking challah onion bread is a real delight.

DIFFICULTY: Hard

PREP TIME: 1 hour

COOK TIME: 30 minutes, plus 3 hours to rest

YIELD: 1 large loaf

DIETARY NOTES: Vegetarian

INGREDIENTS:

1 tablespoon (13 grams) canola oil

2 large onions, thinly sliced

1 teaspoon (4 grams) salt

1½ tablespoons (17 grams) active dry yeast

¾ cup (177 milliliters) water, warmed to 100°F (38°C)

4 cups (585 grams) bread flour, plus more if needed

2 teaspoons (8 grams) salt

¼ cup (54 grams) vegetable oil

¼ cup (84 grams) honey

3 eggs

2 egg yolks, egg whites reserved

White sesame seeds

Black sesame seeds

Heat a medium nonstick pan with the canola oil over medium heat. Toss the onions until coated with the oil. Cook until they turn translucent, about 2 minutes.

Add salt, stir, and reduce the heat to medium-low. Cook, stirring occasionally, until the onions become golden and caramelized, about 30 to 45 minutes. Remove from the heat and set aside to cool.

Combine the yeast and the water in a small bowl. Allow the yeast to bloom and become foamy, about five minutes. Combine the bread flour and salt in a large bowl. Add the yeast water, vegetable oil, honey, 3 whole eggs, and 2 egg yolks. Start to mix it, but before it comes together add the caramelized onions. Continue to mix until the dough just comes together.

Knead the dough for 10 minutes. If the dough is too sticky, add more flour. Shape into a ball and transfer to a large, oiled bowl. Cover and place in a warm area. Let proof for 2 hours, or until doubled in size.

Transfer the dough to a floured countertop and punch down. Divide into 3 equal portions and shape each into a rough tube shape. Cover with a towel and let rest for 15 minutes.

Lightly roll out one piece of dough to a rope 18 inches (46 centimeters) long without using too much pressure. If the dough resists, allow it to rest another 10 minutes. Repeat this with the other 2 portions.

Continued on page 107

Continued from page 104

To braid the dough, lay the 3 ropes vertically. Pinch together the 3 ends farthest away from you and tuck that part under to keep it together. Take the left rope, lift it over the center rope, and lay it down. Take the right rope, lift it over the center rope, and lay it down. Continue to repeat this pattern, switching between left and right until the bread is fully braided.

At the bottom of the dough, pinch the ends together and tuck under the loaf. Transfer the braided dough onto a baking sheet lined with parchment paper. Cover with a kitchen towel and let rise for 1 hour, or until doubled in size.

Preheat the oven to 375°F (191°C). Uncover the dough and brush with the reserved egg whites. Sprinkle white and black sesame over it. Bake for 25 to 30 minutes, or until the bread is golden brown and reaches 190°F (88°C) on an instant-read thermometer.

FREAKIN' GRATITUDE

◆

Most realms seem to have a native lamb-based specialty dish, and here is Svartalfheim's most popular one. My familiarity with this wonderful leg of lamb recipe colored my overall view of Dwarven meat dishes ... and thus, Brok's crude grilling techniques really threw me for a loop. His idea of "barbecue" was to toss unseasoned slabs of flesh on a heap of coals until they were blackened yet oozing.

Even meat purists prefer a bit of seasoning. This recipe calls for slow-cooking a spice-rubbed leg of lamb for tenderness, and then adds a final quick-searing step to crisp the fat. You can still tear off great hunks with your teeth, Brok style, if you want. But at least they taste good.

DIFFICULTY: Medium

PREP TIME: 30 minutes, plus 1½ hours to rest

COOK TIME: 2 to 2½ hours

YIELD: 8 servings

DIETARY NOTES: Dairy-Free, Gluten-Free

◆

INGREDIENTS:

4½ pounds (2 kilograms) leg of lamb

⅓ cup (50 grams) Dwarven Spice Mixture (page 16)

5 cloves garlic, minced

1 tablespoon (3 grams) fresh thyme

1 tablespoon (6 grams) lemon zest

¼ cup (52 grams) olive oil

2 teaspoons (8 grams) salt

1½ cups (355 grams) vegetable stock

Take the leg of lamb out of the refrigerator 1 hour before cooking. Adjust the oven rack to the middle-lower position. Preheat the oven to 350°F (177°C).

Combine the Dwarven Spice Mixture, garlic, thyme, lemon zest, olive oil, and salt. Rub onto the lamb, making sure to cover it completely.

Place the leg of lamb in a Dutch oven and pour in the vegetable stock. Cover, place in the oven, and cook until the lamb reaches the desired temperature on an instant-read thermometer:

135°F (57°C) FOR MEDIUM-RARE, 1 hour covered, then 30 minutes uncovered

140°F (60°C) FOR MEDIUM, 1½ hours covered, then 30 minutes uncovered

Remove from the oven and let rest for 30 minutes. Increase the oven temperature to 500°F (260°C). Move the oven rack up about two levels. Place the Dutch oven in the oven, uncovered. Cook until the fat begins to crisp up, about 5 to 10 minutes. Flip the lamb and repeat for the other side.

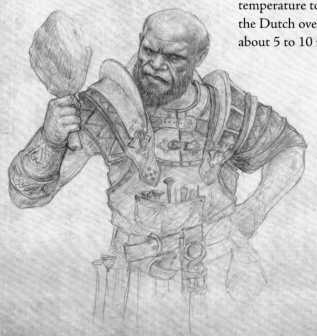

SAUSAGE ROLLS

◆

If ever a food item was destined for Dwarf consumption, this is it. Sausage rolls stuffed with ground beef and lamb are one of Svartalfheim's greatest recipe exports. Also known across the realms as Miner's Delight, this meaty entrée is the kind of filling feast that tastes so good, you can't help but overeat just a bit. Or maybe a bit more.

Once when I was in Svartalfheim for a metalworking festival, an event that excites Dwarven folk, I ended up in a beer garden with a crowd of blacksmith's apprentices. Brew after brew was hoisted high, and many high-minded oaths were sworn. Some Dwarves spoke of slights they'd suffered from Gods or Elves. After another round of beer, the temperature rose further, and these young ones were ready to march against Asgard or Alfheim to prove the superiority of Dwarven ways.

Just as the swagger was getting out of hand, a Dwarf maiden glided up with a huge platter of sausage rolls perched on her shoulder. Another server followed with a big cloth-covered basket of challah onion bread. Once those hit our tabletop, the braggadocio ended abruptly, replaced by a feeding frenzy that slowly morphed into contented moans and murmurs of camaraderie. Sausage and bread had tamed the war beast.

DIFFICULTY: Hard

PREP TIME: 1 hour, plus 30 minutes to cool and rest

COOK TIME: 1½ hours

YIELD: 8 servings

DIETARY NOTES: N/A

IN COLLABORATION WITH:
Estelle Tigani

◆

INGREDIENTS:

1 tablespoon (13 grams) olive oil

1 medium onion, finely chopped

2 medium shallots, finely chopped

1 carrot, peeled and finely chopped

5 cloves garlic, minced

1 pound (454 grams) ground beef

1 pound (454 grams) ground lamb

2 eggs

⅓ cup (95 grams) ketchup

1¼ cup (68 grams) panko bread crumbs

⅓ cup (40 grams) fresh parsley, finely chopped

2 teaspoons (8 grams) salt

1 tablespoon (4 grams) Spartan Spice Mixture (page 19)

1 tablespoon (8 grams) ground fennel

2 teaspoons (4½ grams) black pepper

4 puff pastry sheets, defrosted

Heat a medium nonstick pan with the olive oil over medium-high heat. Add the onions, shallots, and carrots. Sauté until softened, about 5 minutes. Add the garlic and cook for another 2 minutes.

Transfer to a large bowl and let cool completely. Add the ground beef and lamb, 2 eggs, ketchup, panko, parsley, salt, Spartan Spice Mixture, fennel, and pepper. Mix until well combined.

Place the sheets of puff pastry in a row with a 1-inch (2½-centimeter) overlap between each of them. Press down with a rolling pin to fuse the edges together.

Place the meat mixture near the bottom across the 4 sheets. Leave about 8 inches (20 centimeters) on one side and 4 inches (10 centimeters) on the other side empty. This is for the head and tail respectively.

Tightly roll the sausage roll up from the bottom. Pinch the puff pastry together along the seam. Turn the pastry so the seam side is on the bottom.

IF THERE IS A LOT OF EXCESS PASTRY ON THE SIDES AFTER ROLLING IT, REMOVE IT. BAKING THIS WITH TOO MUCH PUFF PASTRY WILL LEAVE THE PASTRY A BIT RAW.

Continued on page 112

EGG WASH:

1 egg

2 tablespoons (30 mililiters) water

Continued from page 111

Carefully transfer the log onto a large baking sheet with parchment paper. Place the tail down first, then make a circle with the log, making sure the overlapping layer doesn't have any meat. Carefully shape the tail end into a pointy tail and shape the head end to match the serpent's head. Place in the freezer for 10 minutes.

Preheat the oven to 350°F (177°C). To make an egg wash, whisk together the egg and the water in a small bowl. Remove the baking sheet from the freezer. Brush the shaped sausage roll on the top and sides with the egg wash. Bake for 1 hour 15 minutes, or until the top is golden brown and the meat is cooked through. If the ends start to brown too quickly, cover with aluminum foil as it cooks. Let cool for 10 minutes before cutting open.

FISH BANH MI

◆

ere's another great fish recipe I learned from Dafraeg, the surly guy who ran the kitchen for the Dwarven Council. You can use several different catches, but I prefer salmon for this amazing fish sandwich. The key to the garlic mayonnaise is to use black garlic! I've never tasted such a perfect condiment.

DIFFICULTY: Medium

PREP TIME: 1 hour, plus 6 hours to marinate

COOK TIME: 30 minutes

YIELD: 4 sandwiches

DIETARY NOTES: N/A

◆

INGREDIENTS:

PICKLED VEGETABLES:

¼ cup (60 grams) rice vinegar, plus more if needed

1 teaspoon (5 grams) fish sauce

1 cup (237 milliliters) warm water

2 tablespoons (32 grams) sugar

1 tablespoon (10 grams) salt

4 cloves garlic, smashed

1 carrot, peeled and julienned

1 medium shallot, julienned

½ small daikon radish, peeled and julienned

SALMON:

¾ cup (170 grams) soy sauce

½ cup (130 grams) mirin

2 teaspoons (12 grams) fish sauce

3 teaspoons (15 grams) sugar

2 teaspoons (8 grams) garlic powder

1 teaspoon (3 grams) ginger powder

1 teaspoon (3 grams) Chinese Five-Spice Mixture (page 20)

Pinch of nutmeg

1¼ pounds salmon, cut into 4 portions

GARLIC MAYONNAISE:

3 cloves (20 grams) black garlic, crushed

⅓ cup (77 grams) mayonnaise

1 teaspoon lime zest

Juice of ½ lime

FOR SANDWICH ASSEMBLY:

½ cup (112 grams) unsalted butter, at room temperature

1 tablespoon (12 grams) garlic powder

1½ teaspoons (3 grams) salt

1 teaspoon (2 grams) black pepper

1 scallion, minced

2 loaves French bread, cut into four 6-inch sandwich portions

1/2 bunch of cilantro

1 cucumber, sliced

2 jalapeños, sliced

Continued on page 116

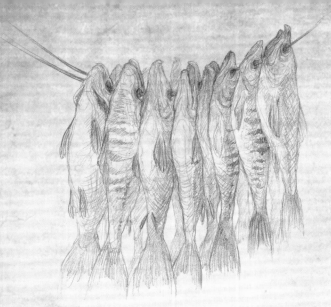

Continued from page 115

To make the pickled vegetables: Combine the rice vinegar, fish sauce, warm water, sugar, salt, and garlic in a large airtight container. Add the carrots, shallots, and radish. If the vegetables are not covered, add more rice vinegar. Refrigerate for at least 4 hours. They can be stored in the refrigerator for about 2 weeks.

To make the salmon: In an airtight bag, combine the soy sauce, mirin, fish sauce, sugar, garlic powder, ginger powder, Chinese Five-Spice Mixture, and nutmeg. Add the salmon and marinate in the refrigerator for at least 6 hours, and up to 24 hours.

Preheat the oven to 400°F (204°C). Place the marinated salmon on a baking sheet and bake for 18 minutes.

Remove and discard the salmon's skin. Flake the salmon into large chunks. For the sandwich, the salmon can be served warm or cold.

To make the garlic mayonnaise: Mash the black garlic in a bowl until smooth. Whisk in the remaining ingredients. Store in an airtight container in the refrigerator for up to 1 week.

To make the sandwiches: Preheat the oven broiler. Combine the butter, garlic powder, salt, pepper, and scallions in a small bowl. Spread the inside of the bread with the butter mixture. Place under the broiler on a baking sheet and toast until the bread has crisped up, about 2 minutes.

To assemble each banh mi, spread the bottom half of the bread with one-fourth of the garlic mayonnaise. Place one-fourth of the cilantro, cucumbers, and salmon on it. Top with one-fourth of the pickled vegetables and jalapeños. Serve immediately.

THE LONGER THEY ARE LEFT TO PICKLE, THE MORE FLAVORFUL THE VEGETABLES WILL BECOME. I HIGHLY RECOMMEND GIVING THESE AT LEAST 24 HOURS FOR A REAL PUNCH.

BABKA BUNS

◆

——————————————————

Don't be fooled by this sweet, braided pastry's cute, flippant name. A lot goes into a babka bun—a lot of work, a lot of flavors, and a *lot* of chocolate filling. So much good comes out of the experience too. I love making these buns almost as much as I love eating them. For me, the actions of creating and eating them become meditations that bring calmness and joy. A platter of warm babka buns, served at the right moment, can help avert many bad things. That's Dwarven wisdom for you.

DIFFICULTY: Hard

PREP TIME: 30 minutes, plus 2 hours to rest

COOK TIME: 20 minutes

YIELD: 6 buns

DIETARY NOTES: Vegetarian

◇

INGREDIENTS:

DOUGH:

½ cup (116 grams) oat milk, warmed to 100°F (38°C), plus more as needed

½ tablespoon (5 grams) active dry yeast

2¾ cups (400 grams) all-purpose flour, plus more if needed

1 tablespoon (7 grams) matcha

3 tablespoons (46 grams) sugar

1 teaspoon (4 grams) salt

2 eggs

1 teaspoon (5 grams) vanilla extract

½ teaspoon (2 grams) almond extract

6 tablespoons (84 grams) unsalted butter, at room temperature

FILLING:

¼ cup (56 grams) unsalted butter

¼ cup (56 grams) dark chocolate, bar or chips

2 tablespoons (18 grams) unsweetened 100% cocoa powder

⅓ cup (45 grams) powdered sugar

1 teaspoon (4 grams) salt

½ cup (67 grams) black sesame seeds, ground

SYRUP:

3 tablespoons (44 mililiters) water

¼ cup (50 grams) sugar

To make the dough: Combine the oat milk and yeast in a small bowl. Allow the yeast to bloom, about five minutes. Combine the flour, matcha, sugar, and salt in a large bowl. Add the yeast mixture, eggs, vanilla extract, and almond extract. Continue to mix until it just comes together.

As you begin to knead the dough, add the butter 1 tablespoon at a time. Knead the dough for 5 minutes. If the dough is too sticky, add 1 tablespoon of flour at a time. If it is too dry, add 1 tablespoon of oat milk at a time. Transfer to a large, oiled bowl, cover, and let rest for 1 hour, or until it has doubled in size.

To make the filling: Melt the butter in a medium saucepan over medium heat. Add the remaining ingredients and mix until the chocolate is melted, about three minutes. Remove from the heat and set aside.

Transfer the dough to a lightly floured countertop and punch down. Lightly knead for 1 minute. Divide into 6 equal portions and cover with a kitchen towel.

Take one of the portions and roll it out into an 8-by-5-inch (20-by-12½-centimeter) rectangle. Using a spoon, spread a generous portion of the filling on the dough, leaving a ¼-inch (6-millimeter) border. Tightly roll the dough into an 8-inch long tube, and pinch the seam to seal.

Cut the roll in half lengthwise, but not all the way through, leaving one end connected on the bottom. Turn the cut ends upward. Tightly braid the two pieces together and pinch the ends together. Shape the braided log into a tight circle, and knot the two ends closed. Place on a baking sheet with parchment paper, leaving 3 inches (7½ centimeters) between each bun. Repeat steps 5 and 6 with the remaining portions.

Continued on page 120

Continued from page 119

Cover the tray with a kitchen towel and allow the buns to rest for 1 hour, or until risen.

To make the syrup: Mix together the water and sugar in a small saucepan over medium-high heat. Once the sugar dissolves, reduce the heat to medium-low and simmer for 10 minutes. Remove from the heat and set aside to cool, 15 to 20 minutes.

Preheat the oven to 350°F (177°C). Brush each bun with the syrup. Bake for 20 minutes, or until golden brown.

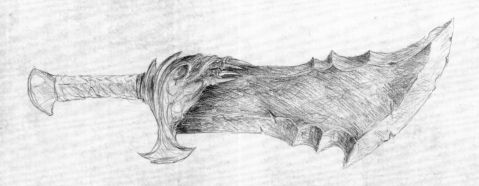

JÖTUNHEIM

Homeland of the Jötnar, this mountain-ous realm is both breathtaking and heartbreaking. Odin's savage war on the Giants, led by his son Thor, has devastated the race. Wielding mighty Mjölnir, the Aesir God of Thunder slaughtered hosts of Jötunn folk, including many Giants in Midgard who'd been invited there by Mortals to hunt the abundant game.

In the beginning, Odin's vendetta against Jötunheim seemed petty; the Jötnar held no particular grievance against the Aesir. The Giants wanted only to be left alone. But Asgard's Long War against Vanaheim teetered back and forth so precariously, Odin feared that any outside alliance with the Vanir—whether Giants, Dwarves, Elves, Mortals, or even mindless beasts—could tip the scales in favor of his enemies. When the Huldra brothers gifted Odin with their lethal hammer, he handed it to Thor with the order to unleash its bloody fury on all Aesir foes.

Then the All-Father began to hear of Jötunn prophecies about Ragnarök, and his paranoia took an even darker, more savage turn. He began to covet the Jötnar's gift of prognostication, longing to foresee the outlines of the apocalypse and avert it somehow . . . or at least escape it. He'd heard only rumors of prophecies, and his incomplete understanding was that Giants—all Giants—would rise up, destroy the gods, and usher in a fiery apocalypse that would immolate the cosmos.

That's when I felt it was time to step in and mediate.

I arranged a summit with the Jötnar ruling council. As a sign of good faith, Odin and I traveled to Jötunheim alone, with no retinue. En route, he assured me of his commitment to peaceful solutions, and swore that in the future, Mjölnir would be used only in defense. I hadn't yet learned how totally

untrustworthy he'd become . . . or how, unhinged by fear of his doom at Ragnarök, my Aesir king was growing ever more desperate and ruthless.

The summit, of course, was a disaster. Odin's true purpose, it turned out, was to covertly surveil the sacred Jötnar prophecy murals in the mountaintop council chamber. The Giants, who never trusted him, caught him spying and cast him out with powerful magicks designed to banish him from Jötunheim forever. In response, Odin unleashed Thor and Mjölnir on the Giant hunting parties in Midgard.

Over time, the All-Father's obsession with Ragnarök morphed into a belief that simply killing off all Giant-kind might stave off the doomsday of the gods. Following this twisted logic, he sent waves of Aesir warriors into all accessible realms, joining Thor in a full genocidal rampage. Giants died in droves trying to resist.

Feeling terrible about diplomacy's wretched failure, I did everything I could to help the Jötnar. We blocked all routes to Jötunheim via my temple's realm travel room, and hid the Jötunheim travel tower in the Realm Between Realms.

Today, according to Mimir and Kratos, Jötunheim is all but deserted, existing only as a somber memorial and graveyard.

I find this particularly sad because few races have such a deep and inspiring trove of lore. Start with the Giant Ymir, the first being who emerged from the void. Legend says every god, mortal, and beast rose from the violent spilling of his mystic life blood.

This includes Bergelmir the Beloved, who rode the torrent of Ymir's "magical guts" (as Mimir calls them) all the way to the land he named Jötunheim. There, he fathered the race of Jötnar, became their first king, and led them to peace and prosperity.

I know plenty of Giants' tales, shared by Jötnar seers over their traditional olive bread, taro stew, and braised beef short ribs called galbijjim, all washed down with a brass-lined drinking horn of mead. My own favorites are the stories of the two Giants who stayed behind in Aesir-overrun Midgard—"the serpent and the guardian"—who served as protectors of all other Giants retreating to Jötunheim:

Laufey the Just. The great Giantess warrior and seer, guardian of Giants, first owner of the Leviathan axe, wife of Kratos and mother of Atreus—the lad who everyone now assures me is remarkable. Sadly, Laufey has passed into spirit and ash. Her deadly skill with Leviathan made her the stuff of nightmares for frightened Aesir warriors. And her ability to see the future rivaled even the visionary sorceress, Gróa the Knowledge Keeper, the first Giantess to see how Ragnarök would unfold. Kratos and Atreus told Mimir that Laufey (known as "Faye" to them) foresaw nearly every step of their journey to Jötunheim, and in fact guided them with her own hand.

Jörmungandr. The inconceivably huge World Serpent, wrapped around Midgard. They say his titanic battle with Thor at Ragnarök shook Yggdrasil so violently that the tree splintered, casting the serpent backward through time to a moment before his own birth … i.e., before our time now! His plummet into the Lake of Nine caused the Great Flood that devastated miles of shoreline and completely submerged my temple. When I contemplate this mind-bending lore, I find myself reflexively uncorking a cask of beer.

Back in the day, if the Jötnar trusted someone who wasn't a Giant, they offered that person what they called the "gift of sight"—special Bifröst crystals for their eyes. The Bifröst energy infused in these glowing lenses let the wearer see hidden things, and travel between the Nine Realms at will.

Very few have been blessed with this remarkable gift; I was honored to be one of them. Another was Mimir.

Today, I feel at a loss at how to return this honor. I guess the least I can do is cook a hearty Jötunn meal for my friends: venison stew, or maybe a nice beef stifado, well browned and slow-cooked with apple dumplings for dessert.

TARO STEW

Not everybody knows what taro is, but if you love cooking, you should. This sweet root vegetable with a nutty flavor is like a hybrid potato-chestnut. Giants not only love taro in soups and stews but also consider it a sacred plant and a symbol of good health. I've seen Jötunn murals depicting ancient, solemn ceremonies around a cauldron labeled with runes containing an offering of taro stew. Back when Giants were flourishing, you could always find this dish on Jötunheim dinner tables during the solstice holidays.

DIFFICULTY: Easy

PREP TIME: 15 minutes

COOK TIME: 45 minutes

YIELD: 4 servings

DIETARY NOTES: Gluten-Free

INGREDIENTS:

4 taros, peeled and cut into large cubes

4 cups (946 grams) chicken broth

1 tablespoon (13 grams) ghee

½ medium red onion, chopped

8 cloves garlic, minced

1 bunch of cilantro

5 Swiss chard leaves, stemmed and roughly chopped

¼ cup (59 mililiters) water, plus more if needed

Juice of 1 lemon

Salt

Black pepper

Place the taro cubes and chicken broth in a medium pot over medium-high heat. Bring to a boil and then reduce the heat. Simmer until the taro is tender, about 20 to 25 minutes.

While the taro cooks, heat the ghee in a medium nonstick frying pan over medium heat. Add the onions and cook until softened, about 5 to 8 minutes. Add the garlic and cook until the onions are golden brown, about 5 minutes. Transfer to a blender.

In the same pan, place the cilantro, Swiss chard, and water. Cover and cook until the chard just wilts, around 3 to 5 minutes. Transfer to the blender with the onions and garlic. Pulse until smooth. If the mixture is too thick and not blending, add a few tablespoons of water.

When the taro is done, add the blended ingredients, mix well, and let it heat through. Add the lemon juice. Season with salt and pepper.

STIFADO

Moist-heat cooking with a Dutch oven is a big part of Jötunn cuisine. Giants liked their meats slow-cooked, tender, and well-infused with the cleverly balanced spice mixes in the cooking juice. This beef stew dish is so flavorful that I inevitably frustrate my dinner partners because I eat it far too slowly, savoring every bite. Kratos will say: "Can we move on to the next course, Týr?" Brok would fold his arms and glare at me. I find it amusing. Back in the old days, nobody ever complained because, as the Aesir God of War, I typically outranked everybody at the table. Those days are long gone, but I can still choose to eat my stifado just as I want.

DIFFICULTY: Medium

PREP TIME: 45 minutes

COOK TIME: 3 hours

YIELD: 5 servings

DIETARY NOTES: Dairy-Free, Gluten-Free

INGREDIENTS:

1½ pounds (680 grams) beef chuck, cut into 1-inch (2½-centimeter) cubes

2 teaspoons (10 grams) salt

1 teaspoon (2 grams) black pepper

1 tablespoon (15 milliliters) canola oil

1 medium onion, sliced

5 cloves garlic, sliced

1 tablespoon (7 grams) Spartan Spice Mixture (page 19)

1 teaspoon (3 grams) cumin

1 teaspoon (5 grams) sugar

Pinch of ground allspice

Pinch of ground nutmeg

2 tablespoons (28 grams) tomato paste

2 tablespoons (30 grams) red wine vinegar

1 cup (240 grams) red wine

28 ounces (793 grams) canned crushed tomatoes

1 cup (240 grams) beef broth

1 bay leaf

1 cinnamon stick

2 pounds (907 grams) shallots, peeled and left whole

Season the beef with the salt and pepper. Heat a medium Dutch oven with canola oil over medium-high heat. Add a single layer of the beef, but do not overcrowd. Brown all sides of the meat, about 5 to 8 minutes. Remove and place on a plate. Add more canola oil and continue this process with all the beef.

Add the onions and, if needed, more canola oil. Sauté the onions until softened, about 5 to 8 minutes. Add the garlic, Spartan Spice Mixture, cumin, sugar, allspice, and nutmeg. Cook for another 2 minutes. Add the tomato paste and mix well.

Add the beef and any juices on the plate and stir together with the red wine vinegar, red wine, crushed tomatoes, beef broth, bay leaf, and cinnamon stick. Bring to a boil and then reduce the heat to low. Let simmer for 2 hours.

Just before the 2-hour cook time finishes, heat a medium pan over medium-high heat. Add the whole shallots and cook until golden, about 8 to 10 minutes. Transfer to the Dutch oven and stir. Simmer for another 45 minutes until the meat is tender.

IF YOU CAN'T FIND SHALLOTS FOR THIS RECIPE, PEARL ONIONS ARE A FINE REPLACEMENT.

GALBIJJIM

Back when Jötnar folk still roamed the realms, the origin of this marvelous short ribs dish was often debated in taverns. The traditional story credits the version to Skaði, the great Jötunn huntress and bow-master. The legendary Queen of the Hunt could track down any game, especially in winter; she glided over snow in her makeshift skis, fashioned from the long ribs of pack animals. Once home, she'd spend hours trying new ways to cook up her latest kill.

Most likely, Skaði's recipe was first fashioned for braising wild boar short ribs, which are excellent; she was certainly the wild boar's bane in her day. But the more popular version that spread like wildfire (or maybe a grease fire?) through realm kitchens uses beef short ribs.

DIFFICULTY: Medium

PREP TIME: 30 minutes, plus 15 minutes to soak

COOK TIME: 5 hours

YIELD: 6 servings

DIETARY NOTES: Dairy-Free

INGREDIENTS:

3 pounds (1.3 kilograms) beef short ribs

Salt

Black pepper

2 tablespoons (30 mililiters) canola oil

1-inch (2½-centimeter) piece of ginger, julienned

4 cloves garlic, chopped

2 scallions, white parts only, chopped

1 medium Korean radish, peeled, quartered, and sliced into ½-inch (1¼-centimeter) pieces

1 large onion, cut into large slices

4 carrots, cut into 1-inch (2½-centimeter) pieces

5 shiitake mushrooms, quartered

1 medium Korean pear, cut into bite-sized pieces

½ cup (120 grams) soy sauce

½ cup (120 grams) mirin

2 tablespoons (30 grams) sugar

2 tablespoons (30 grams) light brown sugar

Soak the beef ribs in a bowl of cold water for at least 15 minutes to remove the excess blood. Dry them thoroughly. Season with salt and pepper.

Heat a Dutch oven over medium-high heat with 2 tablespoons of canola oil. Add a single layer of short ribs, but do not overcrowd. Brown all sides of the meat, 5 to 8 minutes per batch. Remove and place on a plate. Add more canola oil and continue this process for all of the beef.

In the Dutch oven, add more canola oil, ginger, and garlic and cook for about 3 minutes. Add the Korean radish, onions, and carrots. Mix to coat them with the oil and cook until the vegetables are slightly softened, about 5 to 8 minutes.

Preheat the oven to 250°F (121°C). Add the short ribs, shiitake mushrooms, and Korean pear. In a medium bowl, combine the soy sauce, mirin, and both sugars. Pour into the Dutch oven and mix until everything is slightly coated in the sauce.

Cover and place in the oven for at least 4 hours. Check and stir every 90 minutes.

THE LONGER YOU COOK THIS, THE MORE TENDER THE MEAT WILL BE. I COOK MINE FOR 5 HOURS TO MAKE THE PERFECT BITE.

VENISON STEW

◆

Back before my recently-ended incarceration, I would regularly accompany Jötunn hunting parties to northern Midgard. The Mortals of that region had taken my culture-sharing initiatives to heart, inviting other races to hunt the game-rich forests around the Lake of Nine. Deer were so plentiful there that almost any party was likely to bag several pouches of venison.

Thus, the Giants began to experiment with different ways to prepare the meat. As mentioned earlier, the Jötunn people were quite fond of stews, soups, and other slow-cook methods for meat dishes. This tasty venison stew recipe became a staple of hunters on the move because it's so easy—all you need is a good pit of campfire coals, a cast iron Dutch oven with a solid handle, and a sack of simple, pre-prepared spices and other ingredients. Keep in mind, it tastes just as good when made in the warm confines of your home kitchen too!

DIFFICULTY: Easy

PREP TIME: 45 minutes

COOK TIME: 6 hours

YIELD: 4 servings

DIETARY NOTES: Dairy-Free

◆

INGREDIENTS:

½ cup (82 grams) all-purpose flour

2 teaspoons (8 grams) salt

14 juniper berries, crushed

2 tablespoons (8 grams) Jötunn Spice Mixture (page 15)

2 teaspoons (4 grams) black pepper

3 pounds (1.3 kilograms) venison stew meat, cut into large cubes

2 tablespoon (30 milliliters) canola oil

3 medium onions, thinly sliced

1 medium red onion, thinly sliced

⅓ cup (20 grams) light brown sugar

4 cloves garlic, minced

3 carrots, peeled and cut into bite-sized pieces

2 cups (473 grams) beef broth

2 tablespoons (22 grams) potato starch

2 cups (473 grams) stout beer

1 bay leaf

2 purple sweet potatoes, peeled and cut into large cubes

Preheat the oven to 300°F (149°C). Combine the flour, salt, juniper berries, Jötunn Spice Mixture, and pepper in a large sealable bag. Place the venison in the bag, seal, and shake to coat.

Heat a Dutch oven with canola oil over medium heat. Add a single layer of venison, but do not overcrowd. Brown all sides of the meat, 3 to 5 minutes. Remove and place on a plate. Add more canola oil and continue this process for all of the venison.

Add the white and red onions and, if needed, more canola oil. Sauté the onions until caramelized, about 15 minutes.

Add the brown sugar and garlic. Cook for 2 minutes.

Add the venison and any juices on the plate. Stir together. Add the carrots. Cook for 3 minutes.

Combine the beef broth and potato starch in a medium bowl and whisk until smooth. Add to the Dutch oven and stir.

Pour the stout into the Dutch oven and stir. Finally, add the bay leaf. Cover, place in the oven, and cook for 3 to 5 hours, until the meat is tender. During the last 30 minutes of cooking, uncover and add the sweet potatoes.

VEGETABLE STEW

Giants loved meat dishes, but their cooks could do amazing things with produce too. This vegetable stew recipe mixes potatoes with ten other types of delicious veggies. Hence its amusing "insider" name—in Jötunheim kitchens, it was jokingly referred to as Starkaðr Stew. Starkaðr the Mighty, of course, was the towering warrior of Jötnar legend. Eight arms, two legs—many fearsome appendages—all trained to swing a broad sword! Though legend remembers Starkaðr as a formidable warrior, he was also a cunning strategist.

When word of Starkaðr's fighting prowess began circulating, Odin was furious. The Giants were peaceful, pliable, and that's how Odin liked them. Even Mimir made the mistake of telling Odin, "If the Giants ever have anything so organized as an army, Starkaðr would be leading the charge." Fuming, Odin dispatched his strongest Einherjar troop to hunt down the Giant. However, Starkaðr knew Odin was coming for him and already had a plan.

Einherjar were known to never pass a mead hall, so Starkaðr set one up right on their path. He made his vegetable stew, but it had a secret ingredient—a powerful sleeping potion. The Einherjar slurped down the stew and fell into a deep slumber. Starkaðr then trashed the hall to make it look like a terrible fight had taken place. After days with no word, Odin sent ravens to report and was shocked to learn that Starkaðr had bested his entire troop, leaving them unconscious. Though Odin would never admit it, he became fearful of Starkaðr the Mighty from that day on.

DIFFICULTY: Easy

PREP TIME: 30 minutes

COOK TIME: 1 hour

YIELD: 6 servings

DIETARY NOTES: Vegan, Gluten-Free

INGREDIENTS:

2 tablespoons (26 grams) olive oil

1 onion, chopped

2 celery stalks, chopped

3 carrots, peeled and chopped

Salt

Black pepper

1 leek, white and light green part only, chopped

5 cloves garlic, minced

One 6-ounce can (170 grams) tomato paste

2 teaspoons (9 grams) sugar

1 tablespoon (6 grams) Spartan Spice Mixture (page 19)

1 teaspoon (3 grams) Curry Spice Mixture (page 23)

2 teaspoons (2 grams) dried rosemary

One 14½-ounce (411-gram) can diced tomatoes

4 cups (946 milliliters) vegetable broth

3 red potatoes, peeled and chopped into large chunks

1 rutabaga, peeled and chopped into large chunks

1 zucchini, cut into large chunks

6 ounces (170 grams) green beans, chopped

6 ounces (170 grams) spinach

Heat a large pot with the olive oil over medium-high heat. Add the onions, celery, and carrots and sauté until the vegetables soften, about 8 minutes. Season generously with salt and pepper. Add the leeks and garlic, stir, and cook until the leeks soften, about 2 minutes.

Add the tomato paste, sugar, Spartan and curry spices, and rosemary. Stir until well combined. Add the diced tomatoes and vegetable broth.

Add the potatoes and rutabaga chunks. Bring to a boil and reduce the heat to medium-low. Simmer for

20 minutes. Add the zucchini and green beans and simmer for another 20 minutes, or until the potatoes and rutabaga have cooked through.

Add the spinach and cook until it wilts, around 3 minutes. Season with more salt and pepper.

OLIVE BREAD

On my list of favorite breads, Jötunn olive sits at the very top with Dwarven challah onion. I was surprised to learn that olive groves are abundant in Jötunheim's coastal hills, where long, dry, warm summers help the trees produce plenty of fruit. With equal parts of Kalamata and green olives, the Giant's version of olive bread has a satisfying balance to its flavor.

DIFFICULTY: Medium

PREP TIME: 30 minutes, plus 3 hours to rest and time to cool

COOK TIME: 45 minutes

YIELD: 1 loaf

DIETARY NOTES: Dairy-Free

INGREDIENTS:

3½ cups (530 grams) all-purpose flour, plus more if needed

2 teaspoons (8 grams) salt

1 tablespoon (4 grams) Spartan Spice Mixture (page 19)

1 tablespoon (14 grams) sugar

2 teaspoons (8 grams) active dry yeast

1½ cups (301 grams) warm water

⅓ cup (56 grams) Kalamata olives, quartered

⅓ cup (65 grams) green olives, quartered

1 tablespoon (13 grams) olive oil

Combine the flour, salt, Spartan Spice Mixture, sugar, and yeast in a large bowl.

Pour the water in the bowl and mix until the dough just comes together. If it is too sticky, add more flour. Lightly knead for three minutes. Fold in both types of olives.

Brush a large bowl with some of the olive oil and place the dough in it. Brush the top of the dough with the remaining oil. Cover and let the dough rise at room temperature for 2 hours.

Remove the dough from the bowl, lightly knead, and shape into a ball. Place on a piece of parchment paper and cover with a kitchen towel for 1 hour.

After the dough has risen for 30 minutes, preheat the oven to 425°F (218°C). Place an empty Dutch oven with a lid in the oven and heat for 30 minutes.

Transfer the dough with the parchment paper into the heated Dutch oven. Cover with the lid and bake for 25 minutes. Remove the lid and bake for another 10 to 20 minutes, or until the loaf is golden brown. Place the bread on a wire rack to cool completely before cutting.

APPLE DUMPLINGS

Sometimes "dessert" is much more than just a sweet end to a meal. Concocting these incredible apple dumplings is an experience so unique, it should exist in its own realm. I really love the hands-on baking process—working my fingers through flour, butter, sugar, salt, and cardamom, then adding water to build perfect dough balls. Not to mention, filling and wrapping the apples and preparing the buttery vanilla sauce. Every step is a treat for the senses!

DIFFICULTY: Medium

PREP TIME: 1 hour, plus 1½ hours to chill

COOK TIME: 1 hour and 20 minutes

YIELD: 8 dumplings

DIETARY NOTES: Vegetarian

INGREDIENTS:

CRUST:

2½ cups (290 grams) all-purpose flour

1 tablespoon (15 grams) sugar

1 teaspoon (3 grams) ground cardamom

1 teaspoon (3 grams) salt

1 cup (224 grams) unsalted butter, cold and cubed

½ cup (105 grams) cold water, plus more if needed

FILLING:

2½ tablespoons (43 grams) sugar

2 teaspoons (5 grams) ground cinnamon

½ teaspoon (2 grams) ground allspice

Pinch of ground nutmeg

6 tablespoons (84 grams) unsalted butter, at room temperature

⅓ cup (50 grams) pecans, roughly chopped

⅓ cup (45 grams) dried cherries, chopped

8 small baking apples, peeled and cored

SAUCE:

1 cup (200 grams) dark brown sugar

1 cup (237 milliliters) water

1 teaspoon (3 grams) salt

3 tablespoons (52 grams) unsalted butter

1 teaspoon (5 grams) vanilla extract

To make the crust: Combine flour, sugar, cardamom, and salt in a medium bowl. Add the butter. Using your hands, combine the butter and the flour. Work it until it resembles a coarse meal, with chunks of butter throughout.

Slowly add the water. If the dough is too dry, add 1 tablespoon of extra water at a time. Combine the mixture and do not overwork it. Form into 8 balls and wrap each in plastic wrap. Refrigerate for at least 1 hour.

To make the filling: Mix the sugar, cinnamon, allspice, nutmeg, butter, pecans, and dried cherries until well combined. Take each of the apples and fill the center with the filling using a spoon or your hands.

Take one of the dough balls and roll out on a floured counter to ⅛ inch (¼ centimeter) thick. Place an apple in the center and wrap the dough around the apple. If there is excess dough at the top, remove it. Press together to seal and smooth the dough around the apple. Transfer to a buttered 9-by-13-inch (33-by-23-centimeter) deep baking dish. Repeat with the remaining apples and dough.

Place the pan with the prepared apples in the refrigerator to rest for 30 minutes.

To make the sauce: Combine the brown sugar, water, salt, and butter in a medium saucepan over medium-high heat. Cook until the sugar has dissolved, about 5 minutes. Add the vanilla extract and set aside.

Preheat the oven to 425°F (218°C). Bake the dumplings for 15 minutes. Remove from the oven, reduce the heat to 350°F (177°C), and pour the sauce over the dumplings. Bake for another 45 to 60 minutes, until the apples are cooked through.

I PERSONALLY LIKE TO DO STEPS 3 AND 4 ONE APPLE AT A TIME. I PEEL AND CORE AN APPLE, STUFF IT, AND THEN WRAP IT.

MUSPELHEIM

This realm of primordial fire and brimstone is home to the fearsome Fire Giants, descendants of their great and terrible leader, Surtr the Brave. Glowing lavafalls cast an eerie luminosity beneath skies blackened by volcanic ash. The lore says Muspelheim isn't just a blazing inferno, but actually the "cradle of fire"—the very source of all heat and light in the cosmos, including the sun and stars and everything that burns. Surtr himself is said to be nearly as ancient as Ymir, the first being to emerge from the void of Ginnungagap.

Sindri tells me Kratos and his son Atreus actually visited Muspelheim several times, primarily to sharpen their combat skills and liberate the Valkyrie Gondul from Odin's corruptive magic. The duo never encountered Fire Giants but found a shrine to Surtr—a classic Jötunn triptych. Its carvings depict Surtr forging a mighty fire-sword, brighter than the sun, and then wielding it against both Odin and Thor on the ash-fields of Ragnarök.

According to our lore master Mimir, Surtr always knew he was doomed to lose this battle, but not before burning Asgard into a heap of embers and ruin. Legend says Surtr waited patiently in Muspelheim, training daily in his realm's flame and ash— perfecting his sword skills, never resting, never sleeping, preparing for the inevitable clash. To stay sharp, the fiery Muspel leader devised a series of impossible combat trials called Surtr's Gauntlet that slalom up the slope of an active volcano.

"To truly embrace your purpose," says Mimir, "and the patience and sacrifice it demands, is to ensure your day will come."

Jötnar prophecy always said Surtr and his Fire Giant minions would remain unseen until the bloody red dawn of Ragnarök. Even so, I actually spoke with Surtr the Brave when finalizing the link to Muspelheim from my temple's realm travel room. At least I *think* it was Surtr; I couldn't see through the wall of flame and smoke. Beyond sealing a formal agreement to open Muspelheim's travel tower, I'd also secretly hoped to crack open a channel of communication with the Fire Giant race.

Oddly enough, Surtr was surprisingly cordial. Trust me, it isn't easy to engage in a businesslike conversation with the prophesied agent of your own doom. But you see, I didn't disagree with Odin's belief that Ragnarök was not inevitable, that it could be neutralized somehow. Truly, I believe any war can be averted. And back then, as I said before, I believed, perhaps vainly, in my own powers of persuasion. I'd had my share of success in negotiating terms of truce across realms.

Of course, I knew Surtr's deep hatred of the Aesir gods would be difficult to counteract. He'd witnessed Odin's cunning and the savagery of my race. Still, I believed in mediation. I believed that sharing knowledge and culture was the surest path to peace. Doomsayers who see holocaust as not only inevitable but also a "cleansing" event are weak-minded cowards, in my view. If I could make inroads into Surtr's realm and undercut the general notion that "prophecy" inevitably determines outcomes . . . well, it was worth a shot.

Also, I was curious what a Fire Giant meal was like. What do these beings eat?

In the end, my meeting with Surtr—or the disembodied voice of Surtr—was brief and pointed. But I did gain one small insight into Muspel culture. When I somewhat impulsively offered to share a drink from my flask of ginger green tea, Surtr's response was: "Isn't ginger too spicy for you Aesir?"

W hen Fire first met Ice in the great void of Ginnungagap, exploding into the stuff of all things, the nascent, elemental flames settled in Muspelheim.

So, if you're one of those culinary purists who insist on grilling your meat only over authentic primordial fire, Muspelheim is your place. All of my Muspel-inspired recipes sizzle in some way. The best vegetable quinoa is charred under a hot broiler and seasoned with a Chinese Five-Spice blend for a numbing, peppery note. And you've never really tasted shishito peppers until you've sampled them blistered.

Chase it all down with a nice ginger green tea. Then sit back and contemplate Surtr and his Fire Giants bringing the cosmic heat.

YAKITORI

I can think of no better reflection of Muspel culture (if you can call a volcanic wasteland "culture") than a tray of flame-broiled chicken and scallion skewers, flame-broiled. Yakitori is simple cooking, even the salty-sweet tare sauce is easy to throw together. And the flavor imbued by the grill is something even a Fire Giant might find "smoky good."

DIFFICULTY: Easy
PREP TIME: 15 minutes
COOK TIME: 45 minutes
YIELD: 5 skewers
DIETARY NOTES: Dairy-Free

INGREDIENTS:

⅔ cup (153 grams) soy sauce

⅓ cup (73 grams) mirin

⅓ cup (73 grams) sake

1 tablespoon (16 grams) light brown sugar

2 tablespoons (43 grams) honey

4 cloves garlic, crushed

2 ½-inch slices ginger

10 scallions, white and light green parts cut into 1-inch (2½-centimeter) pieces

1½ pounds (680 grams) chicken thighs, boneless and skinless, cut into 1-inch (2½-centimeter) cubes

Salt

Black pepper

Soak 5 wooden skewers in water for 30 minutes. Meanwhile, combine the soy sauce, mirin, sake, brown sugar, honey, garlic, ginger, and dark green part of 3 scallions in a medium saucepan. Bring to a boil. Reduce heat to low and let simmer until it reduces by half, about 30 minutes.

Generously salt and pepper the chicken thighs. Place a piece of dark green or white scallion on a skewer. Add a piece of chicken thigh. Continue alternating pieces of scallion and chicken until you fill up the skewer, ending on a scallion. Repeat with the remaining skewers.

Preheat the grill. Cook the skewers for 8 to 10 minutes over the hot side of the grill, flipping to crisp all sides.

BLISTERED SHISHITO PEPPERS

I'm as adventurous as the next food lover. But frankly, the first time I heard the name of this dish, I prepared myself for pain. As it turns out, blistered peppers aren't nearly as scary as they sound. Yes, they're certainly peppery, and the curry spice mix adds a piquant layer on top. But the grilled peppers are so delicious, and the citrus oils of the lemon-lime zest both enhance the flavor and neutralize some of the heat. Still, I enjoy seeing the slightly uneasy response of dinner guests when they see Blistered Shishito Peppers on the banquet menu.

DIFFICULTY: Easy

PREP TIME: 10 minutes, plus 30 minutes to soak skewers

COOK TIME: 5 minutes

YIELD: 5 servings

DIETARY NOTES: Vegan, Gluten-Free

INGREDIENTS:

8 ounces (227 grams) shishito peppers

3 tablespoons (40 grams) olive oil

Zest of 1 lemon

Zest of 1 lime

2 teaspoons (5 grams) Curry Spice Mixture (page 23)

2 teaspoons (6 grams) sesame seeds

Soak 6 wooden skewers in water for 30 minutes. Skewer the peppers on two skewers, keeping the skewers about 1 to 1½ inches (2½ to 4 centimeters) apart.

Preheat the grill. Cook the skewers for 2 to 5 minutes on the hot side of the grill, flipping to crisp both sides.

Combine the olive oil, lemon and lime zest, and curry powder in a medium bowl. Remove the shishito peppers from the skewers and toss in the bowl.

Transfer to a plate and top with sesame seeds.

USING TWO SKEWERS HELPS KEEP THE SHISHITO PEPPERS FROM FLIPPING AROUND WHEN TURNING THE SKEWERS.

GRILLED WHOLE RED SNAPPER

The grilling procedure for this citrus-and-herb-stuffed red snapper makes this dish incomparable. I first tasted it while planning the menu for a Jötnar banquet. Here's what happened: One day, a Jötnar known as Thrym the Cunning (ironic in retrospect) arrived at the banquet in question proudly boasting that he had stolen Thor's hammer, Mjölnir. Thrym told anyone who would listen and attracted quite an audience while he was at it. He started out by claiming that he managed to come upon Thor napping on a Midgard riverbank. Thrym said he snuck in close, snatched Mjölnir from a snoring Thor, and hustled away to a vault he had hidden away in Jötunheim.

As soon as one of the other banquet guests asked if Thrym was concerned about antagonizing Odin himself, he spun a tale about that, too. The boastful Thrym claimed that Odin had sent Freya to him, but she wasn't alone, and Thrym knew the God of Thunder was hiding in her retinue. Odin's plan was to have Thor sneak into Jötunheim and kill every Giant in the realm. But Thrym was smart and cunning, and he demanded that Thor reveal himself as soon as Freya approached.

Thrym laughed as he regaled the crowd that Thor begged to have Mjölnir back, shocked that Thrym was able to uncover their plan, and Freya begged for forgiveness. To apologize, Freya supposedly cast a mighty spell that hurled Thor out of Jötunheim for good just before she left as well. As Thrym helped himself to a second serving of the banquet meal, he claimed he deserved heaping praise for his actions, insisting that he, Thrym the Cunning, saved countless Giants from a bloody demise.

I don't believe any of Thrym's story to be true, but it did spread far enough that Asgard's spies heard it, and the All-Father took pieces of it to further his public perception.

One final note: I placed this wonderful snapper recipe along with the tale of Thrym the Cunning in the Muspelheim section of this cookbook for a reason. Word is, when Surtr heard Odin's version of the story, his sizzling hatred for everything Asgardian grew even hotter in its intensity. Any doubts the Fire Giants may have had regarding their role in Ragnarök were burned away for good!

DIFFICULTY: Medium

PREP TIME: 15 minutes, plus 30 minutes to rest

COOK TIME: 20 minutes

YIELD: 4 servings

DIETARY NOTES: Dairy-Free, Gluten-Free

Continued on page 148

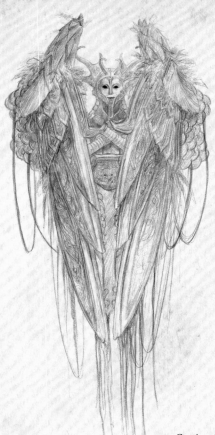

Continued from page 147

INGREDIENTS:

2 pounds (907 grams) whole red snapper, cleaned and scaled

2 tablespoons (30 ml) olive oil

Salt

Black pepper

1 lemon, thinly sliced

1 lime, thinly sliced

3 sprigs fresh dill

3 sprigs fresh tarragon

Remove the red snapper from the refrigerator and let rest at room temperature for 30 minutes. Pat the fish dry, inside and out. Rub the fish with the olive oil. Season with salt and pepper.

Stuff the cavity with lemon and lime slices, dill, and tarragon.

 Preheat the grill. Rub the grates with any neutral oil. Place the red snapper directly over the heat and cook for 10 minutes, until the bottom side crisps.

Carefully flip the fish and cook over the direct heat for another 8 to 10 minutes, until this side also crisps up. If the fish has not reached an internal temperature of 135°F (57°C), move off the direct heat, cover, and cook until done using indirect heat.

MAKE SURE NOT TO MOVE THE FISH DURING THIS INITIAL COOK, OR ELSE THE SKIN MIGHT TEAR.

CHARRED VEGETABLE QUINOA

◆

Quinoa is so rich in nutritional value, but for years I struggled to find ways to include it in recipes to my satisfaction. Then one evening, I accidentally charred a broiler pan of chopped, spiced vegetables. On a whim, I tossed them into a well-fluffed bowl of quinoa, added a little olive oil and spice . . . and they were absolutely delicious! So here, in the spirit of the realm, I include this well-charred recipe.

DIFFICULTY: Easy

PREP TIME: 45 minutes

COOK TIME: 45 minutes

YIELD: 6 to 8 servings

DIETARY NOTES: Vegan, Gluten-Free

◇

INGREDIENTS:

CHARRED VEGETABLES:

1 zucchini, cut into ½-inch (1¼-centimeter) slices

1 squash, cut into ½-inch (1¼-centimeter) slices

1 eggplant, cut into ½-inch (1¼-centimeter) slices

2 bell peppers, cut into ½-inch (1¼-centimeter) pieces

1 bunch of asparagus, cut into 1-inch (2½-centimeter) pieces

1 red onion, thinly sliced

2 tablespoons (26 grams) olive oil

1 teaspoon (2 grams) Chinese Five-Spice Mixture (page 20)

Salt

Black pepper

QUINOA:

2 cups (473 mililiters) water

Pinch of salt

1 tablespoon (13 grams) olive oil

1 cup (185 grams) quinoa

¼ cup (52 grams) olive oil

1 tablespoon (6 grams) Spartan Spice Mixture (page 19)

To make the vegetables: Preheat the oven to 425°F (218°C). Combine the zucchini, squash, eggplant, bell peppers, asparagus, and red onion in a large bowl. Add olive oil and toss together. Prepare a baking sheet with aluminum foil and nonstick spray. Place the mixed vegetables on the sheet and evenly sprinkle with the Chinese five-spice. Generously season with salt and pepper. Bake for 20 to 25 minutes, or until the vegetables have browned. Remove from the oven and set aside to cool.

To make the quinoa: Heat a small pot with the water over medium-high heat. Bring the water to a boil and add the salt and olive oil. Add the quinoa, cover, reduce heat to low, and let simmer for 15 minutes. Remove from the heat and let rest, covered, for 5 minutes.

Transfer the cooked quinoa into a large bowl. Add the olive oil and Spartan Spice Mixture and mix to coat the quinoa. Add the charred vegetables and toss until well combined.

TO GIVE THE VEGETABLES AN EXTRA CHAR, AFTER THEY'RE COOKED THROUGH LEAVE THEM UNDER A HOT BROILER FOR 2 MINUTES. MAKE SURE TO KEEP AN EYE ON THEM BECAUSE THEY WILL CHAR QUICKLY AT THIS POINT.

GINGER GREEN TEA

◆

This concoction may be the most refreshing beverage I've ever sipped Even served alone, a well-steeped sencha is a perfectly good libation, and green tea is certainly beneficial for one's health. But when you add the ingenious ginger cinnamon syrup . . . well, the drink rises to a higher level of satisfaction. Note that you can serve ginger green tea after it initially cools, but the flavor is much richer if you stash the pitcher in cold storage overnight before serving.

DIFFICULTY: Easy

PREP TIME: 30 minutes, plus 8 hours to chill

COOK TIME: 40 minutes

YIELD: 6 servings

DIETARY NOTES: Vegetarian, Gluten-Free

◆

INGREDIENTS:

GINGER CINNAMON SYRUP:

1 cup (237 mililiters) water

½ cup (170 grams) honey

1 teaspoon (4 grams) ginger powder

½ teaspoon (2 grams) ground cinnamon

4-inch piece of ginger, peeled and sliced

1-inch (2½-centimeter) piece of turmeric, peeled and sliced

1 cinnamon stick

TEA:

3 tablespoons (21 grams) loose-leaf sencha

7 cups (1.65 liters) water, plus more if needed

To make the syrup: Combine all the ingredients in a saucepan and place over medium-high heat. Stir until the sugar has dissolved and then bring to a boil. Reduce the heat and simmer for 10 minutes. Remove the turmeric and simmer for another 20 minutes. Remove from the heat and strain through a fine mesh strainer into a pitcher.

To make the tea: Heat 7 cups of water in a large pot over medium-high heat until it reaches 175°F (79°C) on an instant-read thermometer. Add the sencha and steep for 3 to 5 minutes. Strain the tea leaves, transfer the water into the pitcher with the ginger cinnamon syrup, and stir. To make your tea slightly less sweet, add more hot water.

Let cool completely and refrigerate overnight before serving.

RED VELVET CRÈME BRÛLÉE

◆

This crème brûlée is one of my more complicated dessert recipes. But if, like me, you've come to find joy in the sensual adventure of cooking—for example, preparing the filling to just the right consistency, or holding the flame over the crème brûlée just so—you'll love the creation almost as much as the consumption. Not to mention, your kitchen will smell heavenly for hours. Note: Be sure to use a sturdy set of ceramic ramekins. They must withstand not only high oven temperatures but also the flame of a cooking torch when you caramelize the sugar on top.

DIFFICULTY: Hard

PREP TIME: 45 minutes, plus an hour to cool and at least 3 hours to chill

COOK TIME: 45 minutes

YIELD: 6 servings

DIETARY NOTES: Vegetarian, Gluten-Free

◇

INGREDIENTS:

30 fresh cherries, pitted and quartered

¼ cup (28 grams) unsweetened 100% cocoa powder

½ cup (170 grams) honey

2 drops red food dye

2 teaspoons (7 grams) vanilla extract

1 teaspoon (4 grams) salt

7 egg yolks

2 cups (465 grams) heavy cream

¼ cup (60 grams) sugar, plus more for topping

I PERSONALLY LIKE TO LET THESE CHILL OVERNIGHT FOR THE BEST RESULTS.

Preheat the oven to 325°F (163°C). Evenly split the cherries between 6 ramekins.

Combine the cocoa powder, honey, food dye, vanilla, salt, and egg yolks in a large bowl. Combine heavy cream and sugar in a saucepan over medium-high heat. Let simmer for 10 minutes. Carefully and slowly pour the heated cream into the bowl while constantly whisking. Split between the 6 prepared ramekins.

Place the ramekins inside a deep baking dish. Fill the dish with water about halfway up the side of the ramekins. Bake for 35 to 45 minutes, or until the edges are set but the centers jiggle slightly and have reached an internal temperature of 175°F (79°C) on an instant-read thermometer. Remove the ramekins from the baking dish and let them cool to room temperature. Then refrigerate the ramekins for at least 3 hours.

Before serving, sprinkle the top of the crème brûlées with sugar. Use a torch to melt and caramelize the sugar until amber in color.

HELHEIM

Helheim is home to the inglorious dead. The Valkyries, before being corrupted by Odin, had a sacred vocation: to cull the souls of warriors who die honorably in battle and escort them to the great banquet hall of Valhalla. All other souls end up trooping into Helheim. Thus, if your death is shameful or even just ordinary, your soul is cast into a wind-blasted, bitterly cold hellscape where you wander aimlessly in bleakest despair until the dawn of Ragnarök. I find it hard to comprehend such a fate. Or see the fairness of it.

I've met these souls. Other than Dwarves who can slip in and out of any realm unnoticed, very few living people have actually visited Helheim and returned. Mimir says Kratos and his son are members of this select group. Years ago, I utilized the Helheim tower on the Lake of Nine to test our realm travel connection, which I suspected few would ever use. As I crossed the ice-covered travel bridge and stepped through Helheim's outer gate into the dead realm, I found myself surrounded by a host of souls.

It was a terrible encounter. Many had grievances or unfinished business in life. They groped desperately, moaning, and beseeching me to help them settle their affairs. As I pulled away, I tried to envision their ghostly existence. Every one of these spirits had once walked a path—whether filled with love, hate, hope, or despair—with some sort of purpose, even if simply to survive another day. Then that path suddenly ended, and here they are in Helheim.

I saw myself as one of them. For years, maybe centuries, I wandered aimlessly in this truly godforsaken place. *Why am I here?*

Then a great moment comes, one that finally bestows purpose: *Ragnarök!* On that apocalyptic day, decreed by inscrutable Norns, the spinners of fate, to be the doomsday of Gods and Mortals, my pathetic blue soul suddenly burrows upward from Helheim. It erupts like a frigid fountain on the field of Vígríðr, site of the great final battle. I hear the great Gjallahorn calling warriors to ranks. Surtr and Muspelheim's fierce Fire Giants join Helheim's hordes (including my tiny, insignificant soul) on one side, while Gods and Mortals, Elves and Dwarves, and the warrior spirits of Valhalla align on the other. The clash of armies is like a clap of cosmic thunder, so titanic that Yggdrasil shudders. All Nine Realms are shaken.

I find it an altogether depressing scenario. The injustice of conscripting legions of lost souls into the meat grinder of war never sits right with me. I see no glory in that. My instinct is to gather the decision-makers from all sides, sit them down at a table piled high with food and drink, and then hammer out a simple, peaceful resolution. But apparently, the machinations of Ragnarök defy such solutions.

As I write this, I sit surrounded by remnants of a meal I prepared for Kratos and others. Mimir is here too, but he doesn't eat, for obvious reasons.

I gladly took over cooking duties from Kratos after several unpleasant attempts to consume a food item he tried to pass off as "simple Spartan fare." Tonight, my squid ink pasta with scallops was a big hit. I didn't tell anyone I learned the recipe from a vaporous, moaning spirit I met on the bridge beyond the Gate of Helheim, not far from where the powerful Máttugr Helson, Ice Troll born in Hel, once stood guard. The poor ghost just wanted to speak of his previous life as a fishmonger in the marketplaces of Midgard's River Pass, back before the Great Flood sent his soul to the frozen realm. He also passed along a recipe for a fruit-topped meringue that I hope to try soon. It might be a bit light for my crusty crew, but I include it here for you.

The way things are going, I might run into that fishmonger any day now, maybe right out in the yard! As the post-Ragnarök cosmos continues to settle out and reform, Helheim's blue hosts continue to crawl out of the permafrost and Hel Tears. My theory is that these returnees are particularly tortured souls drawn back to the lands of their corporeal existence by a deep sense of loss . . . or worse, a cold core of righteous anger.

Each one probably wonders: *Why me?* As would I. Frightening as they are, I do feel empathy for them.

In any case, nothing seems to settle my mind quite like cooking. As Mimir and others bring me up to speed on these things that have happened—such huge, apocalyptic things I've missed!—I choose to remember how much joy there is to be found in the little things. Things like preparing a tricky cheese and leek soufflé. That's on the menu for tomorrow night, assuming we don't get killed by angry Hel-Walkers before then.

ASTRID'S CHEESE & LEEK SOUFFLÉ

To start, let me be clear: There are no "recipes" per se in Helheim. Nobody cooks food there. It's a world of forlorn, vapory ghosts. Yet all these entities were once living people, made of flesh, who got hungry, and enjoyed good food. And, as I mentioned above, I did actually learn some of these recipes in Helheim! Others I found elsewhere or formulated myself, and then adapted to the essence of the dead realm.

This soufflé recipe is a good example. Technically, my source was a living Mortal woman, a shopkeeper named Astrid I once met in a River Pass marketplace. I spoke with her at length about some runestones and a strange serpent's scale in her display case. Her asking prices were quite high, many hundreds of hacksilver, but I purchased a stone anyway. She was so delighted she immediately invited me to dine with her family in their residence above the shop.

Upstairs, Astrid began preparing the very cheese and leek soufflé recipe that I offer here. When I asked if I could help, she resisted at first, claiming that "guests should never lift a finger for their meal." But when I explained how deeply I enjoy cooking, Astrid tossed me an apron! The recipe was complex and tricky to execute—timing was everything—and I loved every minute of it. That humble meal with Astrid's family was one of the most enjoyable I've ever eaten.

The next time I came through River Pass, about a year later, I stopped in Astrid's shop again and learned she'd been killed by Reavers in a robbery. I closed my eyes and pictured that good woman's ghost consigned to the frozen plazas of Helheim, wandering in a daze and wondering what she'd done to warrant such a fate. I was absolutely devastated. Astrid deserved so much better.

The very least I can do is memorialize her beloved recipe here and invoke her name.

DIFFICULTY: Very Hard

PREP TIME: 45 minutes

COOK TIME: 40 minutes

YIELD: 5 soufflés

DIETARY NOTES: Vegetarian

INGREDIENTS:

4 tablespoons (56 grams) unsalted butter

3 tablespoons (45 grams) Parmesan cheese, finely grated

1 tablespoon (13 grams) olive oil

2 leeks, white and light green parts only

Salt

Black pepper

4 tablespoons (45 grams) all-purpose flour

1½ cups (344 grams) milk

3 egg yolks

4 egg whites

4 ounces (113 grams) Gruyère cheese, finely grated

Continued on page 160

Continued from page 159

Use 1 tablespoon of butter to grease five 6-ounce (170-gram) ramekins all around the inside. Sprinkle the ramekins with Parmesan cheese. Transfer into the refrigerator while you make the soufflé batter.

Cut one of the leeks into thin slices. Heat a small frying pan with the olive oil over medium-high heat. Add the leek and cook until just crisped, about 4 minutes. Season with salt and pepper.

Melt the remaining butter in a saucepan over medium-high heat. Add the flour while constantly whisking. After the butter and flour have combined into a roux, about 3 to 4 minutes, slowly whisk in the milk until fully combined. Take the other leek and cut it in half. Add it to the saucepan, reduce the heat to low, and cook for 5 minutes, until thickened. Remove the leek from the mixture and discard it. Remove the pan from the heat.

While whisking, add one egg yolk at a time to the mixture. Stir until well combined. Transfer it into a large bowl. Add Gruyère and sautéed leeks and mix until combined. Set aside.

Preheat the oven to 400°F (204°C). Place the egg whites in a medium bowl, or the bowl of a stand mixer. Using a whisk attachment, whip the eggs with a hand mixer or the stand mixer. Whisk until the eggs just reach stiff, firm peaks.

Take a third of the egg whites and whisk them into the batter until well incorporated. Add another third of egg whites and gently fold in until just combined. Add the remaining egg whites and fold them in.

Once combined, spoon the soufflé mixture to the prepared ramekins, filling each about four-fifths of the way up.

Transfer to the oven and reduce the temperature to 375°F (191°C). Bake for 25 minutes. Do not open the oven, as this will cause the soufflés to collapse.

Serve immediately. The moment you take these out of the oven they will begin to deflate.

IT IS VERY IMPORTANT TO MAKE SURE THAT THE RAMEKINS ARE COMPLETELY GREASED. IF YOU SKIMP ON THIS, THE SOUFFLÉS WILL STICK TO THE RAMEKINS.

YOU'VE REACHED THE STIFF PEAK STAGE WHEN YOU CAN TAKE SOME OF THE EGG WHITES ON YOUR WHISK, FLIP IT UPSIDE DOWN, AND THEY STAND UP, HOLDING A PEAK-LIKE SHAPE. MAKE SURE NOT TO OVERMIX THESE—IF THEY BECOME CHUNKY YOU HAVE WHIPPED THEM TOO FAR!

AVOCADO EGGS BENEDICT

This version of the classic benedict dish appears in this chapter due to a sheer coincidence of personal history—I just happened to have it for breakfast on the morning I made my first visit to Helheim. I had no idea what to expect upon arrival and no idea who would meet me, if anyone. The structure of Helheim's ruling hierarchy was (and continues to be) quite mysterious.

Outside Hel's gate, I was swarmed by souls. Inside, I found myself face-to-face with the Mighty Son of Hel, Máttugr Helson. This towering, impassive, immensely powerful Frost Troll approached me slowly, wielding a massive blue totem powered by Hel's energy itself. I knew that Máttugr's job was to maintain the orderly flow of souls across the Bridge of the Damned into Helheim. What I didn't know was that his assignment also included keeping out not-yet-dead interlopers, like me. In his native tongue—which, fortunately, I understood—Máttugr explained that if I wanted to cross the bridge, he'd have to crush me first. His tone was polite, like he was offering to help me.

I declined and hurried back across the realm travel bridge with amazing alacrity. Now, whenever I make this tasty avocado eggs Benedict (which is quite often, frankly), I think of Máttugr 's polite offer.

DIFFICULTY: Medium
PREP TIME: 30 minutes
COOK TIME: 30 minutes
YIELD: 2 servings
DIETARY NOTES: Vegetarian

INGREDIENTS:

AVOCADO HOLLANDAISE:

1 large avocado

1 tablespoon (14 grams) lemon juice

¼ cup (59 milliliters) hot water, plus more if needed

2 tablespoons (26 grams) olive oil

Salt

Black pepper

POACHED EGGS:

2 teaspoons (10 grams) vinegar

Pinch of salt

4 eggs, cracked into four separate small bowls

FOR ASSEMBLY:

2 English muffins, toasted and cut open

Arugula, for topping

Balsamic vinegar, for topping

To make the hollandaise: Combine the avocado, lemon juice, and hot water in a blender until smooth. If the mixture is too thick to pour, add more water to loosen slightly. Continue running the blender on low and slowly add the olive oil. Whisk together until completely combined. Season with salt and pepper.

To poach the eggs: Bring 2 inches of water to a boil in a deep, large pan. Whisk in the vinegar and salt. Carefully take the eggs and slowly pour them in the water. Cook them for 3½ minutes. Carefully flip the eggs and cook for another minute. Remove the eggs and place on a paper towel to dry.

To assemble each eggs Benedict: Place both halves of a toasted English muffin faceup on a plate. Add a handful of arugula and a drizzle of balsamic vinegar to each side. Top each with a poached egg followed by a generous drizzling of the avocado hollandaise sauce.

I RECOMMEND MAKING THIS RIGHT BEFORE YOU SERVE IT. AS THE AVOCADO SITS OUT, IT BEGINS TO OXIDIZE AND LOSE ITS COLOR.

SQUID INK PASTA

◆

As I explained earlier, I learned this dish from a ghost. The odd thing was, the whispery spirit remembered every tiny detail about preparing his squid ink pasta, but when I asked his name in life, his eyes widened, and he moaned that he couldn't remember! I was stunned—his very identity, his self, was somehow fading away, and yet he could recount meticulous details about his fishmonger business, the best way to shuck shellfish, the tide schedules, and of course his marvelous pasta recipe. I began to wonder if such a moment would happen to me someday . . . perhaps in the aftermath of Ragnarök?

DIFFICULTY: Medium
PREP TIME: 15 minutes
COOK TIME: 30 minutes
YIELD: 4 servings
DIETARY NOTES: N/A

◆

INGREDIENTS:

1 pound (454 grams) squid ink pasta

1½ tablespoons (17 grams) salt, plus more for seasoning scallops

1 pound (454 grams) scallops

Black pepper

6 tablespoons (84 grams) unsalted butter

2 tablespoons (26 grams) olive oil

8 cloves garlic, minced

1 medium shallot, minced

1 cup (236 grams) white wine

½ cup (118 milliliters) reserved pasta water

Zest and juice of 2 lemons

Heat enough water to cover the pasta in a large pot over high heat. When it reaches a boil, add 1½ tablespoons (17 grams) of salt. Cook the pasta until just al dente. Drain the pasta and reserve at least ½ cup of the water. Set aside.

Season the scallops generously with salt and pepper. Heat a stainless-steel pan with 1 tablespoon of olive oil over high heat. Add the scallops in a single layer to the pan. Cook until a golden crust forms on the bottom, about 2 to 3 minutes. Flip and cook until golden on that side, about 2 minutes. Place 1 tablespoon of butter in the pan. Baste the scallops with the melted butter and olive oil and cook for about 2 more minutes, until cooked through. Transfer to a plate and let rest.

Add another tablespoon of olive oil to the pan and add the garlic and shallots. Cook until softened, about 2 minutes. Reduce the heat to medium-high and add the white wine. Cook until it reduces by half, about 5 minutes. Add the lemon juice and mix together. Add the cooked pasta. Slowly add the reserved pasta water until the sauce comes together with the pasta. Add the lemon zest.

Split between 4 plates and top with scallops.

DALGONA MATCHA

This is a perfect postprandial cold treat that's so easy to make. All it takes is a little work with the whisk for about three minutes to fluff up the coconut cream and matcha. Then mix it all together and enjoy. I'm told that matcha is healthy, and it provides a delicious boost of energy after a meal. I frequently offer this chilly drink as a tribute to all the cold souls in Helheim: May they all find their peace!

DIFFICULTY: Easy

PREP TIME: 15 minutes

YIELD: 1 serving

DIETARY NOTES: Vegetarian, Gluten-Free

INGREDIENTS:

¼ cup (90 grams) coconut cream, cold

2 teaspoons (7 grams) matcha

1¼ cups (296 milliliters) oat milk

¼ teaspoon (1 milliliter) vanilla extract

1 tablespoon (21 grams) honey

3 to 4 ice cubes

Place the coconut cream in a tall plastic cup that the whisk attachment of a hand mixer can reach the bottom of. Whisk until the cream becomes fluffy and has doubled in size, about 3 minutes. Add the matcha and whisk until just combined.

Combine the oat milk, vanilla extract, and honey in a pint glass. Add the ice cubes. Top with the matcha coconut cream mixture. Serve immediately.

PAVLOVA

◆

Ｔhis amazing dessert with a multi-part construction is complex but satisfying. Getting the details right is important. You build the delicate meringue, whisk the lime curd, whip the cream, and then comes the tricky assembly. Overall, making pavlova calls for a dash of humility. I like that, especially because I learned the value of humility the hard way, long ago.

At one time, I believed my intellect and powers of persuasion to be unmatched in the realms. Then I met Mimir, my first reality check. His brilliance was immediately humbling, and he also helped me see how I'd underestimated Odin's dark intelligence and cunning. Thinking back, I think my visit to Helheim shattered any remaining vanity about my own importance in the cosmic scheme of things. Although I was sure I could hold my own against any grim emissary the cold realm might produce, the horde of lost souls I met outside Hel's gate shook me.

Yes, this chilled white dessert reminds me of Helheim's icy, opaque waters. And with every amazing bite of pavlova, I've learned to enjoy the fullness of life in that exact, fleeting moment!

DIFFICULTY: Hard

PREP TIME: 1 hour, plus 3 hours to cool

COOK TIME: 1½ hours

YIELD: 8 servings

DIETARY NOTES: Vegetarian, Gluten-Free

◇

INGREDIENTS:

MERINGUE:

5 egg whites, at room temperature

1¼ cups (250 grams) sugar

1 teaspoon (5 grams) cream of tartar

1 teaspoon (5 grams) vanilla extract

¼ teaspoon (1 gram) almond extract

1½ teaspoons (5 grams) cornstarch

LIME CURD:

3 egg yolks

½ cup (100 grams) sugar

1 tablespoon (2 grams) lime zest

¼ cup (58 grams) lime juice

Pinch of salt

¼ cup (56 grams) unsalted butter

WHIPPED CREAM:

1¼ cups (270 grams) heavy cream

3 tablespoons (60 grams) powdered sugar

1 teaspoon (5 milliliters) vanilla extract

FOR ASSEMBLY:

2 kiwifruits, sliced

6 ounces (170 grams) blackberries

Continued on page 171

Continued from page 168

To make the meringue: Preheat the oven to 275°F (135°C). Place the sugar in a food processor. Blend for 1 minute to make superfine sugar. Line a baking sheet with parchment paper.

Place the egg whites in a bowl of a stand mixer, or in a large bowl with a hand mixer. Using a whisk attachment, blend at medium-low speed until the eggs start to froth. Increase the speed to high and whisk until it forms soft peaks. Soft peaks will just hold their shape, but the peak will curl downward.

Slowly add the sugar, 1 tablespoon at a time. Introducing the sugar too quickly will cause the mixture to deflate. Blend until the egg whites form stiff peaks.

Add the cream of tartar and vanilla and almond extracts. Whisk until just combined. Fold in the cornstarch until combined.

Transfer to the center of the prepared baking sheet. Shape into an 8-inch (20-centimeter) round. Create a 2- to 3-inch (5- to 7½-centimeter) round dip in the center. With a spatula, shape the sides into chaotic peaks.

Bake for 10 minutes. Reduce the heat to 225°F (107°C) and bake for another 70 to 80 minutes, until the outside is dry and crisp. Turn off the heat and let cool, in the oven, for 2 to 3 hours.

To make the lime curd: In a medium saucepan, whisk the egg yolks, sugar, and lime zest until the sugar dissolves and the mixture is smooth. Add the lime juice and salt. Place over low heat and whisk until it thickens, about 10 minutes.

Add the butter. Whisk until the butter is completely melted. Strain into an airtight, heatproof container and let cool completely. Refrigerate for at least 1 hour before serving, and for up to 1 week.

To make the whipped cream: Place the ingredients for the whipped cream in a bowl and whisk until it forms stiff peaks.

To assemble: Fill the dip in the meringue with the prepared whipped cream. Top with the fruit. Once the meringue is dressed up, serve immediately. Either pour the lime curd directly over the pavlova or serve it separately.

NIΛFHEIM

Niflheim lies at Yggdrasil's roots, just above Ginnungagap, the great void that birthed the cosmos. It is a desolate realm known for its wild icy mists, so intense they once powered the legendary forges of the Dwarven blacksmith, Ivaldi. Today, sadly, these mists are cursed and poisonous. While Niflheim is not as frigid and windswept as its close neighbor Helheim, it is a bitterly cold land where sustenance is sparse. Visitors are advised to pack warm breads, soups, porridge, and other foods that offer comfort in chilly, forbidding places.

(Actually, visitors are advised to *not visit*. But Niflheim's nooks are loaded with such valuable treasures and artifacts that hardy adventurers find the effort worthwhile.)

Some ancient myths portray Niflheim as a world of the "dishonored dead," overrun by Hel's spillover hordes—inhabitants supposedly too evil to be contained by Helheim's snowy wastes. But while Niflheim is certainly rife with unpleasant inhabitants, none I've encountered here are ghostly denizens. Instead, Niflheim seems now to be a land of monsters—Wulvers, Tatzelwurms, the occasional Ogre—along with twisted Revenants, Vikens, some renegade Dark Elves, and other forsaken minions of lost clans. Mimir tells me that even a corrupted Valkyrie, Hildr, once haunted the Niflheim wastes until Kratos and his son liberated her spirit from its debased physical form.

So, how has an entire realm come to be so cursed?

As is so often the case across the Nine Realms, the misery in the region traces directly back to the obsessions of our glorious All-Father, Odin.

My Niflheim story begins with the aforementioned Ivaldi, a renowned inventor and metalwork master. Sindri, who knew Ivaldi well, calls him one of the cleverest Dwarves ever. Seeking a better place for his private workshop, Ivaldi left Svartalfheim with his sons Andvari, Fáfnir, and Mótsognir and wandered into Niflheim.

Once there, Ivaldi discovered a way to harness the wild power of the Niflheim mists, a process that remains a secret to this very day. He used it to fire his forge, then channeled the power into a series of astounding inventions— mechanisms, contraptions, and devices that were said to shock the realms! Other Dwarves immigrated to Niflheim to work for him.

None of this sat well with Odin. The All-Father sees anything that challenges Aesir superiority as a dire threat. Ivaldi, a mere Dwarf, was beginning to displace the gods themselves as a source of authority! Odin, wielding seiðr magic he'd learned from Freya, cast a terrible spell on Niflheim's mists. The curse turned them into a poisonous fog that killed Ivaldi and drove his people, including his sons, from the realm.

Today, anyone who lingers too long in Niflheim's vapors suffers a slow, agonizing death—according to Mimir, "an eternal reminder of Ivaldi's toxic pride." Indeed, the realm's mist is known today as Ivaldi's Curse.

The Sons of Ivaldi, of course, became famous in their own right. All three barely escaped the killer mists of Niflheim and ended up in Midgard.

Andvari set up a lab within the Dwarven tunnels of Völunder Mines and, as Brok explained it, "started tampering with souls, dark rituals, and matters of the night." He tried extracting the souls of Ancients to transform the primeval creatures into a tireless, obedient workforce. Unfortunately, the big soulless monsters went berserk and started slaughtering Dwarf miners to incinerate their souls. Not pleasant at all. Soul Eaters, they're called now—agents of immolating destruction.

173

Mótsognir and his followers settled amongst the fertile farmlands of Veithurgard and established a prosperous, flourishing kingdom under his leadership. Over time, however, he was overcome by an irrational belief that Odin would lay waste to Veithurgard in further retribution for Ivaldi's stand in Niflheim. Mótsognir embarked on an obsessive search for the mystic components of a legendary Dwarven armor called Dvegræðikr, believing it could protect him from Odin's wrath. However, the search ended up decimating his own people. Forced into his stronghold of Konùnsgard, Mótsognir slaughtered his remaining subjects to harvest their screams for the armor. The dead rose as Hel-Walkers and killed their mad king.

The third brother, Fáfnir, turned into an avid "collector" (thief) of artifacts, relics, and other treasures. He traveled the realms, pilfering prizes and stashing them in his well-hidden storeroom. One relic, a special whetstone, was so valued that Fáfnir actually sneaked back into Niflheim to steal it! Thievery proved to be Fáfnir's downfall: One of his stolen relics, a magical Vanir mirror, turned the Dwarf into a dragon. Today, I think more realm travelers know him as Fáfnir the Dragon than Fáfnir, Son of Ivaldi.

Thus did Niflheim's poisons scatter the few Dwarves and Mortals who once settled there. The realm remains cold and forbidding. It's no picnic spot. I certainly wouldn't host a dinner party there.

Yet I continue to believe that Yggdrasil bears Niflheim's weight on her roots for some good reason. I'm no seer, but perhaps the misty land will play a key role in our cosmic future. Whatever the case, I choose to celebrate all nine realms, even this one.

As you prepare and serve the comforting recipes I share in honor of Niflheim, be sure to raise a glass and utter a toast: "In every realm, treasures can be found."

BANANA BREAD MUFFINS

◆

Warm comfort foods are the only way to survive a tour of Niflheim. (Of course, these days it also helps to have a military escort.) This easy recipe yields 12 perfect muffins to provide energy as you dodge Wulvers and slip around roiling clouds of Cursed Mist. Or you could just stay home, eat the muffins, and tell the story of Ivaldi to your children. These days, that would certainly be my preference.

DIFFICULTY: Easy

PREP TIME: 20 minutes

COOK TIME: 23 minutes

YIELD: 12 muffins

DIETARY NOTES: Vegetarian

IN COLLABORATION WITH:
Mallorie Lesher

◆

INGREDIENTS:

2 cups (300 grams) all-purpose flour

1 teaspoon (5 grams) baking powder

½ teaspoon (2 grams) baking soda

½ teaspoon (1 gram) ground cinnamon

½ teaspoon (1 gram) ground cardamom

½ teaspoon (2 grams) salt

½ cup (65 grams) rolled oats

3 very ripe bananas

6 tablespoons (84 grams) unsalted butter, melted then cooled

¼ cup (64 grams) Greek yogurt

½ cup (113 grams) sugar

¼ cup (57 grams) light brown sugar

2 eggs

1 teaspoon (5 grams) vanilla extract

¼ cup (65 grams) buttermilk

Preheat the oven to 375°F (191°C). Combine the flour, baking powder, baking soda, cinnamon, cardamom, salt, and rolled oats in a medium bowl. Set aside.

Place the bananas in a large bowl and mash until smooth. Add the butter, Greek yogurt, both sugars, eggs, and vanilla extract and mix until just combined.

Fold in the flour mixture until it just comes together. Finally, add the buttermilk and mix until just combined. Do not overmix this batter, or the muffins will be dense and tough.

Divide the batter into a 12-cup muffin tin. Bake for 5 minutes. Reduce the heat to 350°F (177°C) and bake for another 15 to 18 minutes, or until golden brown and cooked through, until a toothpick comes out clean.

HONEYCOMB TOAST

Here's another easy, comforting dish. The honeycomb makes it special, hence the name. The ricotta mix provides a perfect flavor combination of sweet and citrus, and a berry topper adds color. According to Kratos, a honeycomb toast breakfast is a great way to kick off a Hel-Walker hunt. Note: My recipe says adding a slice of burrata is optional. But trust me, you definitely want it onboard!

DIFFICULTY: Easy

PREP TIME: 15 minutes

YIELD: 2 servings

DIETARY NOTES: Vegetarian

IN COLLABORATION WITH:
Hannah Filipski

INGREDIENTS:

⅓ cup (80 grams) ricotta cheese

½ tablespoon (7 grams) honey

½ teaspoon (3 grams) lemon juice

½ teaspoon (2 grams) olive oil

Zest of 1 lemon

Pinch of salt

Pinch of black pepper

1 thick slice of Challah Onion Bread (page 104), cut in half

2 slices burrata cheese (optional)

2 tablespoon (34 grams) honeycomb

5 to 7 raspberries

Combine the ricotta, honey, olive oil, lemon juice and zest, salt, and pepper in a bowl. Mix together until smooth. Set aside.

Toast the challah until golden brown. Spread the ricotta mixture on each half-slice. If desired, add a slice of burrata. Top with honeycomb and raspberries.

SOPA DE OSO

◆

Roasted poblano peppers are one of my favorite foods. They're mild enough that I can throw a handful on a grill and blacken them, bringing out the fruity flavors, then peel and eat them plain or with a bit of salt. (Disclaimer: Brok found this disgusting and maintained that only meat belongs on a grill.) This recipe uses blackened poblanos as a base ingredient for the soup, and it's a stunning revelation.

Speaking of Brok, he was initially excited when I told him that in one Midgardian language, *sopa de oso* translates literally as "bear soup." But when he discovered that no bear meat is used, and in fact, the soup is *entirely* meatless he stalked off to one of his workshops and started hammering things.

DIFFICULTY: Medium

PREP TIME: 45 minutes, plus 10 minutes to cool

COOK TIME: 45 minutes

YIELD: 6 servings

DIETARY NOTES: Vegetarian

IN COLLABORATION WITH:
Christian Orellana

IF YOU DO NOT HAVE A GAS STOVE, YOU CAN PLACE THE POBLANO PEPPERS UNDER A BROILER, FLIPPING UNTIL ALL SIDES ARE CHARRED.

◇

INGREDIENTS:

4 poblano peppers

2 tablespoons (26 grams) olive oil

2 medium onions, sliced

4 cloves garlic, minced

1 tablespoon (6 grams) Jötunn Spice Mixture (page 15)

2 teaspoons (2 grams) Mexican oregano

1 teaspoon (4 grams) salt

½ teaspoon (1 gram) black pepper

4 Roma tomatoes, diced

4 medium white potatoes, peeled and cut into large chunks

4 cups (946 milliliters) vegetable broth

1 bay leaf

1 bunch of cilantro, stemmed and chopped

Cotija cheese, for serving

Place the poblano peppers directly on the gas stove over medium heat. Turn and cook until all sides have blackened. Once roasted, transfer onto aluminum foil and wrap shut. Let cool for 10 minutes.

Once the peppers are cooled, remove the skin, and deseed them. Cut them into large strips and set aside.

Heat a medium pot with the olive oil over medium heat. Add the onions and cook until lightly caramelized, about 15 minutes. Add the garlic, Jötunn spices, Mexican oregano, salt, and pepper and cook for another 2 minutes.

Add the tomatoes and cook until they have softened, about 5 to 8 minutes.

Add the potatoes, vegetable broth, and bay leaf. Bring to a boil, reduce heat to medium-low, and simmer for 30 minutes, until the potatoes are cooked through.

Remove and discard bay leaf. Add the cilantro and the poblano peppers and cook for another 5 minutes. Serve with cotija cheese on top.

BERRY CHERRY SODA BREAD

◆

Brok's past protestations to the contrary, it's actually a misconception that Dwarves eat nothing but meat. In fact, all six of my Niflheim recipes are entirely vegetarian, and most of them originated in Dwarven enclaves around Ivaldi's Workshop. For example, I learned this fruit-studded quick-bread recipe from a Dwarf seamstress. I'd been out hunting with Mótsognir, one of Ivaldi's sons, when a hissing Tatzelwurm popped out of the ground and slashed my cloak. After dispatching the beast, Mótsognir sent me to the seamstress, Finellyn, and she offered me tea and a snack while mending my garment.

The snack was a plate of terrific soda bread with a berries and cherries baked in. After the first bite, I leaped to my feet and said, "Finellyn, I'll give you fifty extra hacksilver if you jot this bread recipe on the back of your bill of services!" Pleased, she provided the recipe but refused any payment for it. Her bill of 15 hacksilver for the clothing repair was far too modest as well! So, I insisted that Finellyn accept my gratuity of a silver Elven clasp I'd picked up in Alfheim.

I sometimes wonder if Finellyn was one of the Dwarven folk who escaped Niflheim after Odin poisoned the realm's mists with his evil seiðr spell. I certainly hope so.

DIFFICULTY: Easy

PREP TIME: 20 minutes, plus time to cool

COOK TIME: 1 hour

YIELD: 1 loaf

DIETARY NOTES: Vegetarian

IN COLLABORATION WITH:
Sara Davenport

◇

INGREDIENTS:

½ cup (112 grams) unsalted butter, cubed, room temperature, plus more for greasing pan

3 cups (410 grams) all-purpose flour

1 cup (117 grams) rolled oats

¾ cup (162 grams) sugar

1½ teaspoons (6 grams) salt

1½ teaspoons (4 grams) ground cinnamon

½ teaspoon (1 gram) ground nutmeg

1 tablespoon (13 grams) baking powder

1 teaspoon (6 grams) baking soda

¾ cup (135 grams) dried blueberries

½ cup (75 grams) dried cranberries

½ cup (90 grams) dried cherries

1½ cups (350 grams) buttermilk

1 egg

1 teaspoon (5 grams) vanilla extract

Preheat the oven to 350°F (177°C). Grease a 10-inch (25-centimeter) cast-iron pan with some of the butter. Combine the flour, rolled oats, sugar, salt, cinnamon, nutmeg, baking powder, and baking soda in a large bowl. Add ½ cup cubed butter and combine with your hands until it resembles coarse cornmeal. Add the blueberries, cranberries, and cherries and toss until coated in the flour mixture.

In a small bowl, whisk the buttermilk, egg, and vanilla extract. Pour into the large bowl and stir with a spatula until just combined. The dough will still be wet.

Transfer the dough to the pan. Bake for 45 to 60 minutes, or until a toothpick comes out clean. Cool completely.

ÆBLEKAGE

◆

Here's another dish that I found in Niflheim. I discovered this recipe for Dwarven apple cake at a bakery in the township outside Ivaldi's Workshop. It calls for successive layers of apple filling, a gingersnap crumb mix, and whipped cream. The baker (I didn't get his name, I'm sad to say) told me he originally created this æblekage for a traditional ceremony that officially celebrates the coming-of-age of young folk. But it grew so popular that it became a regular dessert or afternoon snack in the Workshop villages. Note: Æblekage isn't really a cake, as no baking is involved.

DIFFICULTY: Medium

PREP TIME: 1 hour

COOK TIME: 30 minutes

YIELD: 6 servings

DIETARY NOTES: Vegetarian

IN COLLABORATION WITH:
Robert Rappoport

◇

INGREDIENTS:

APPLE FILLING:

5 large apples, peeled, cored, and cut into chunks

⅓ cup (75 grams) sugar

¾ cup (177 milliliters) water

Juice of 1 lemon

Seeds scraped from 1 vanilla bean

Pinch of salt

1 teaspoon ground cardamom

CRUMBLE:

2 cups (200 grams) gingersnap cookies

½ cup (80 grams) hazelnuts

¼ cup (55 grams) sugar

7 tablespoons (98 grams) unsalted butter

WHIPPED CREAM:

1½ cups (340 grams) heavy cream

1½ tablespoons (20 grams) sugar

1 teaspoon (5 grams) vanilla extract

To make the apple filling: Combine all the filling ingredients in a medium pot. Cook over medium heat until the apples have softened, about 20 minutes. Transfer to a large bowl and mash until it's a puree. Set aside and let cool completely.

To make the crumble: Place the gingersnap cookies in a food processor and pulse until small crumbs form. Put the hazelnuts in a sealable bag and mash until lightly crushed. Combine the gingersnap crumbs, hazelnuts, and sugar.

Melt the butter in a large pan over medium heat. Add the crumb mixture, stir constantly, and allow to toast lightly, 3 to 5 minutes. Remove from the heat and let cool completely.

To make the whipped cream: Combine the whipped cream ingredients in a bowl of a stand mixer. Whip on high speed until it forms stiff peaks. If you aren't ready to assemble, cover with plastic wrap and refrigerate.

To assemble: Take one of six containers. Using a spoon, spread a layer of apple puree at the bottom, followed by crumble, and then top with the prepared whipped cream. Repeat until the container is filled. Serve immediately or chill in the refrigerator for at least 4 hours.

I RECOMMEND USING CONTAINERS THAT ARE THE SAME SIZE, SO ALL THE PORTIONS ARE EQUAL. THESE ÆBLEKAGE CAN BE PREPARED HOWEVER YOU WOULD LIKE, SO HAVE FUN WITH IT.

KHÜR RISGRØT

◆

The rich, delicious basmati rice porridge is so easy to make on a cold morning. The recipe originated in Ivaldi's Workshop kitchen. The dish spread widely to the Dwarven refugee colonies that flourished at Völunder, Landsuther, Veithurgard, and elsewhere. Khür risgrøt was particularly popular with Dwarf miners, who worked in tunnels that were often bitterly cold, wet, and miserable.

When I first indulged in this tasty pudding, I was sitting in a large cafeteria with about a hundred tough, hard-bitten miners. I was curious about their underground life and wanted to spend a few days living it. The kitchen staff had gruffly announced the imminent serving of rations. I wasn't expecting much—after all, when one thinks of the word "rations," one usually associates it with tasteless military-style food. But then, out came big bowls of this delightful porridge! I could sense spirits lifting all around me. Good food can be downright medicinal sometimes.

DIFFICULTY: Easy

PREP TIME: 10 minutes, plus 30 minutes to soak

COOK TIME: 45 minutes

YIELD: 4 servings

DIETARY NOTES: Vegetarian

IN COLLABORATION WITH:
Zaid Shaikh

◆

INGREDIENTS:

⅓ cup (70 grams) basmati rice

4 cups (943 grams) milk, plus more if needed

⅓ cup (73 grams) sugar

1 teaspoon (2 grams) ground cardamom

⅔ cup (105 grams) almonds, chopped

1 cup (145 grams) pistachios, chopped

Rinse the rice with water. Place in a medium bowl, cover with water, and let sit for 30 minutes. Drain and set aside.

Heat the milk and sugar in a large pot over medium-high heat. Bring to a boil and reduce the heat to low. Add the rice. Cook until soft, about 30 to 40 minutes.

Add the cardamom, almonds, and pistachios. Stir and cook until thickened. If too thick, loosen it with more milk. Serve warm or chilled.

MAKE SURE TO STIR CONSTANTLY SO THE MILK ON THE BOTTOM OF THE POT DOES NOT BURN.

DIETARY CONSIDERATIONS

	Vegetarian	Vegan	Gluten-Free	Dairy-Free
A Realm Between Realms				
Jötunn Spice Mixture		X		X
Dwarven Spice Mixture		X		X
Spartan Spice Mixture		X		X
Chinese Five-Spice Mixture		X		X
Curry Spice Mixture		X		X
Midgard				
Roast Quail			X	X
Pork Tenderloin			X	X
Hasselbackpoteter	X		X	
Rødkål	X	X	X	X
Mushroom Quiche	X			
Goat Cheese and Apple Tarts	X			
Mulled Apple Juice	X		X	
Alfheim				
Beet Terrine	X			
Mercimekli Köfte	X	X	X	
Spanakopita	X			
Aishi Baladi	X	X		
Kofta			X	X
Spicy Moutabel	X	X	X	
Karkade	X		X	
Vanaheim				
Prosciutto-Wrapped Figs			X	
Shaved Brussels Sprouts Salad	X		X	
Chilean Sea Bass				
Rack of Lamb			X	X
Whole Roasted Carrots	X		X	
Roasted Potatoes	X	X	X	
Baklava Mini Tarts	X			
Ambrosia	X	X	X	
Asgard				
Smoked Salmon Dip				
Lamb Riblets			X	
Kottbullar				

	Vegetarian	Vegan	Gluten-Free	Dairy-Free
Wild Boar Ragú				X
Sockerkringlor	X			
Glogg	X	X	X	
Honeyed Spirits	X		X	
Svartalfheim				
Tuna Tartare				X
Scotch Eggs				
Challah Onion Bread	X			
Freakin' Gratitude			X	X
Sausage Rolls				
Fish Banh Mi				
Babka Buns	X			
Jötunheim				
Taro Stew			X	
Stifado			X	X
Galbijjim				X
Venison Stew				X
Vegetable Stew	X	X	X	
Olive Bread				X
Apple Dumplings	X			
Muspelheim				
Yakitori				X
Blistered Shishito Peppers	X	X	X	
Grilled Whole Red Snapper			X	X
Charred Vegetable Quinoa		X	X	
Ginger Green Tea	X		X	
Red Velvet Crème Brûlée	X		X	
Helheim				
Astrid's Cheese and Leek Soufflé	X			
Avocado Eggs Benedict	X			
Squid Ink Pasta				
Dalgona Matcha	X		X	
Pavlova	X		X	
Niflheim				
Banana Bread Muffins	X			
Honeycomb Toast	X			
Sopa de Oso	X			
Berry Irish Soda Bread	X			
Æblekage	X			
Khür Risgrot	X			

ABOUT THE AUTHORS

VICTORIA ROSENTHAL launched her blog, Pixelated Provisions, in 2012 to combine her lifelong passions for video games and food by recreating consumables found in many of her favorite games. When she isn't experimenting in the kitchen and dreaming up new recipes, she spends time with her husband and corgi hiking, playing video games, and enjoying the latest new restaurants. Victoria is also the author of *Fallout: The Vault Dweller's Official Cookbook*, *Destiny: The Official Cookbook*, *Street Fighter: The Official Street Food Cookbook*, and *The Ultimate FINAL FANTASY XIV Cookbook*. Feel free to say hello on Twitter, Twitch, or Instagram at PixelatedVicka.

RICK BARBA is one of the most published book authors in the videogame industry, with more than 120 game-related titles in print. He co-authored the *God of War Collector's Edition Guide* and also wrote the game's lore book, *God of War: Lore and Legends*.

ᚠᛒᛟᚢᛏ ᛏᚺᛖ ᛁᛚᛚᚢᛊᛏᚱᚨᛏᛟᚱ

ABOUT THE ILLUSTRATOR

IRIS COMPIET is an award-winning artist from the Netherlands. She has worked for a wide range of international clients and contributed to gallery shows and art annuals. She is also the creator of the book *Faeries of the Faultlines*. Drawing inspiration from European folklore, mythology, fairy tales, and the world around her, she strives to open a gateway to the imagination to ignite it even further.

TITAN
BOOKS

144 Southwark Street
London SE1 0UP
www.titanbooks.com

 Find us on Facebook: www.facebook.com/TitanBooks
 Follow us on Twitter: @TitanBooks

A CIP catalogue record for this title is available from the British Library.

ISBN: 978-1-80336-103-1

Special thanks to: Matt Sophos, Rafael Grassetti, Dela Longfish,
Eric Williams, Cory Barlog, Ariel Lawrence, Alison Quirion,
Elize Morgan, Lauren Signorino, Alanah Pearce, Jeff Ketcham,
Carol Chung, and all the aspiring chefs and cooks at Santa Monica Studio

Publisher: Raoul Goff
VP of Licensing and Partnerships: Vanessa Lopez
VP of Creative: Chrissy Kwasnik
VP of Manufacturing: Alix Nicholaeff
Editorial Director: Vicki Jaeger
Designer: Dan Caparo and Lola Villanueva
Design Manager: Megan Sinead-Harris
Senior Editor: Jennifer Sims
Associate Editor: Maya Alpert
Senior Production Editors: Jennifer Bentham and Jan Neal
Senior Production Manager: Greg Steffen
Senior Production Manager, Subsidiary Rights: Lina s Palma-Temena

ROOTS of PEACE   REPLANTED PAPER

Insight Editions, in association with Roots of Peace, will plant two trees for each tree used in the manufacturing of this book.
Roots of Peace is an internationally renowned humanitarian organization dedicated to eradicating land mines worldwide and
converting war-torn lands into productive farms and wildlife habitats. Roots of Peace will plant two million fruit and nut trees
in Afghanistan and provide farmers there with the skills and support necessary for sustainable land use.

Manufactured in China by Insight Editions

10 9 8 7 6 5 4 3 2 1

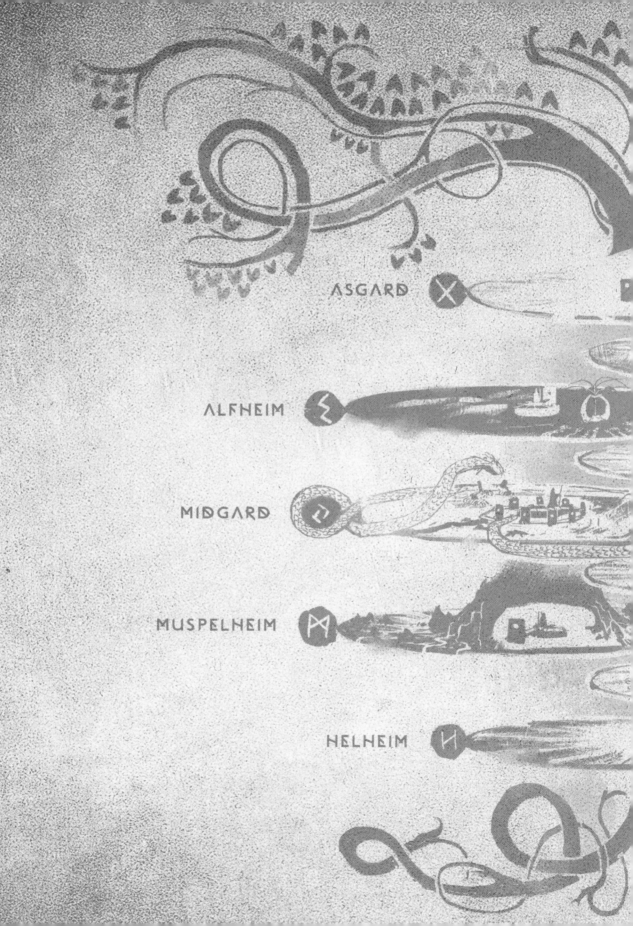

ASGARD

ALFHEIM

MIDGARD

MUSPELHEIM

HELHEIM